BASIC STUDY

OF

HEREROCYCLIC CHEMISTRY

Sanjeev Jena

Lecturer
Department of Chemsitry
Jyoti Vidyalaya Charoda Durg India

LP Inc. Publisher North Carolina USA

July 2015

Although great care has not been taken to provide accurate and current information, neither the author nor the publisher, nor anyone else associated with this publication, shall be liable for any loss, damage, or liability directly or indirectly caused or alleged to be caused by this book. The material contained herein is not intended to provide specific advice or recommendations for any specific situation

First Printing: 2015

ISBN: 978-1-329-34043-5

DEDICATION

To our friends all over the world.

Thank you all.

Without your support and patience, we would have never achieved our dream.

ACKNOWLEDGMENTS

I would like to thank my teachers, my editor, my classmates, and my family without whose help this book would never have been completed.

Thank you for your patience and guidance, your use of the editor's red pen...

Preface to the First Edition

Heterocyclic compounds have a wide range of applications but are of particular interest in medicinal chemistry, and this has catalysed the discovery and development of much heterocyclic chemistry and methods. The preparation of a first edition has allowed us to review thoroughly the material included in the earlier editions, to make amendments in the light of new knowledge, and to include recent work.

We have maintained the principal aim to teach the fundamentals of heterocyclic reactivity and synthesis in a way that is understandable by undergraduate students. However, in recognition of the level at which much heterocyclic chemistry is now normally taught, the book appropriate both for post - graduate level courses, and as a reference text for those involved in heterocyclic chemistry in the work place

The undergraduate student should first read nomenclature , which will provide a structural basis for the chemistry that follows, The student could then proceed to the main chapters, dealing with ' Reactions and Synthesis of … ' in which will be found full discussions of the chemistry of particular systems – pyridines, quinolines, etc.

Sanjeev Jena

Author

CONTENTS

S No	Chapter	Page
1	Introduction	7
2	Nomenclature of heterocyclic compounds	10
3	Furans: Reactions and Synthesis	35
4	Thiophenes: Reactions and Synthesis	50
5	Pyrroles: Reactions and Synthesis	69
6	Pyridines: Reactions and Synthesis	85
7	Indoles: Reactions and Synthesis	111
8	Quinolines and Isoquinolines: Reactions and Synthesis	142

CHAPTER 1

INTRODUCTION OF HETEROCYCLIC

A cyclic organic compound containing all carbon atoms in ring formation is referred to as a carbocyclic compound. If at least one atom other than carbon, forms a part of the ring system then it is designated as a heterocyclic compound. Nitrogen, oxygen and sulfur are the most common heteroatoms but heterocyclic rings containing other hetero atoms are also widely known. An enormous number of heterocyclic compounds are known and this number is increasing rapidly. Accordingly the literature on the subject is very vast. Heterocyclic compounds may be classified into aliphatic and aromatic. The aliphatic heterocyclics are the cyclic analogues of amines, ethers, thioethers, amides, etc. Their properties are particularly influenced by the presence of strain in the ring. These compounds generally consist of small (3- and 4- membered) and common (5 to 7 membered) ring systems. The aromatic heterocyclic compounds, in contrast, are those which have a heteroatom in the ring and behave in a manner similar to benzene in some of their properties. Furthermore, these compounds also comply with the general rule proposed by Hückel. This rule states that aromaticity is obtained in cyclic conjugated and planar systems containing $(4n + 2)$ π electrons. The conjugated cyclic rings contain six π-electrons as in benzene, and this forms a conjugated molecular orbital system which is thermodynamically more stable than the non-cyclically conjugated system. This extra stabilization results in a diminished tendency of the molecule to react by addition but a larger tendency to react by substitution in which the aromatic ring remains intact. A heterocyclic ring may comprise of three or more atoms which may be saturated or unsaturated. Also the ring may contain more than one hetero atom which may be similar or dissimilar.

The chemistry of heterocyclic compounds is as logical as that of aliphatic or aromatic compounds. Their study is of great interest both from the theoretical as well as practical standpoint. Heterocyclic compounds occur widely in nature and in a variety of non-naturally occurring compounds. A large number of heterocyclic compounds are essential to life. Various compounds such as alkaloids, antibiotics, essential amino acids, the vitamins, haemoglobin, the hormones and a large number of synthetic drugs and dyes contain heterocyclic ring systems. A knowledge of heterocyclic chemistry is useful in biosynthesis and in drug metabolism as well. Nucleic acids are important in biological processes of heredity and evolution. There are a large number of synthetic heterocyclic compounds with additional important applications and many are valuable intermediates in synthesis.

CHAPTER 2

NOMENCLATURE OF HETEROCYCLIC

The IUPAC rules allow three nomenclatures.

I. The Hantzsch-Widman Nomenclature.

II. Common Names

III. The Replacement Nomenclature

I.   The Hantzsch-Widman Nomenclature

The Hantzsch-Widman nomenclature is based on the type (Z) of the heteroatom; the ring size (n) and nature of the ring, whether it is saturated or unsaturated . This system of nomenclature applies to monocyclic three-to-ten-membered ring heterocycles.

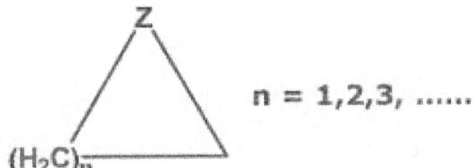

(a) Type of the Heteroatom

The type of heteroatom is indicated by a prefix as shown below for common hetreroatoms:

Table 1: Prefix for hetero Atoms

Hetero Atom	Valence	Prefix
O	2	Oxa
N	3	Aza
S	2	Thia
Se	2	Selena
Te	2	Tellura
P	3	Phospha
As	3	Arsa
Si	4	Sila
Ge	4	Germa

(b) Ring size (n)

The ring size is indicated by a suffix according to Table 2 below. Some of the syllables are derived from Latin numerals, namely ir from tri, et from tetra, ep from hepta, oc from octa, on from nona, ec from deca.

1. **Stems to indicate the ring size of Heterocycles**

Ring Size	Suffix	Ring Size	Suffix
3	ir	7	ep
4	et	8	oc
5	ol	9	on
6	in	10	ec

2. **Stems to indicate the ring size and degree of unsaturation of heterocycles**

Ring Size	Saturated	Unsaturated	Saturated with N
3	-irane	-irine	-iridine
4	-etane	-ete	-etidine
5	--olane	-ole	-olidine
6	--inane	-ine	
7	-epane	-epine	
8	-ocane	-ocine	
9	-onane	-onine	
10	-ecane	-ecine	

According to this system heterocyles are named by combining appropriate prefix/prefixes with a stem from Table II. The letter "a" in the prefix is omitted where necessary. Each suffix consists of a ring size root and an ending intended to

13

designate the degree of unsaturation in the ring. It is important to recognize that the saturated suffix applies only to completely saturated ring systems, and the unsaturated suffix applies to rings incorporating the maximum number of noncumulated double bonds.

Systems having a lesser degree of unsaturation require an appropriate prefix, such as "dihydro"or "tetrahydro" Saturated 3, 4 & 5-membered nitrogen heterocycles should use respectively the traditional "iridine", "etidine" & "olidine" suffix.

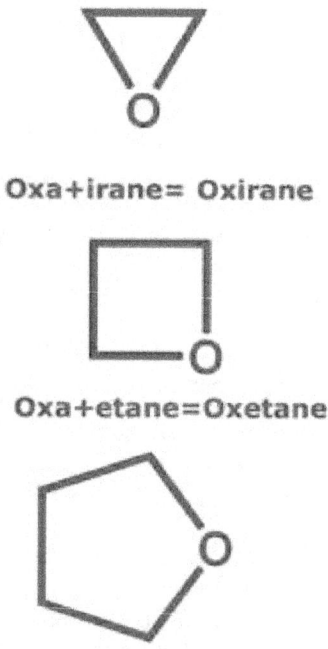

Oxa+irane= Oxirane

Oxa+etane=Oxetane

Oxa+olane= Oxolane

Thia+irane= Thiirane

Thia+etane=Thietane

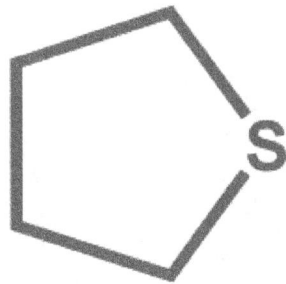

Thia+olane= Thiolane

Aza+iridine= Aziridine

Aza+etidine=Azetidine

Aza+olidine= Azolidine

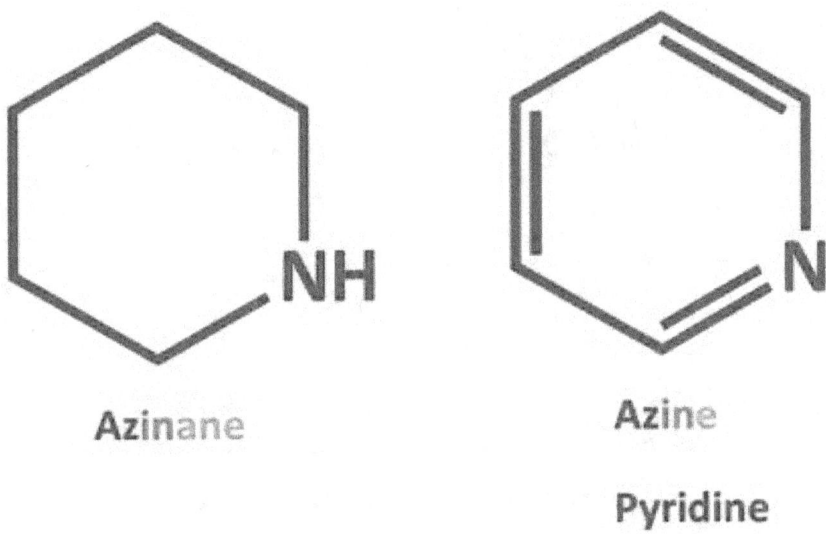

In case of substituents, the heteroatom is designated number 1, and the ubstituents around the chain are numbered so as to have the lowest number for the substituents.

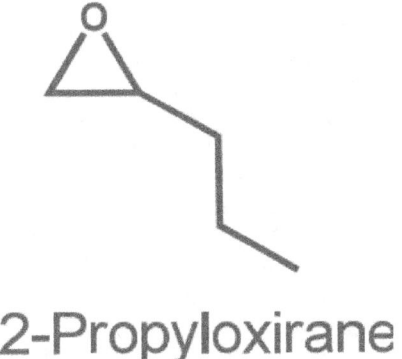

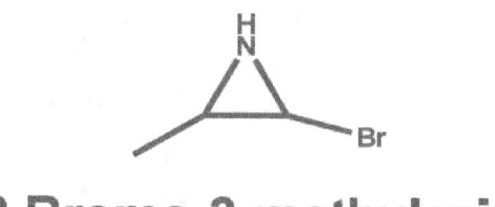

2-Bromo-3-methylaziridine

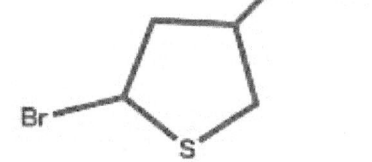

2-Bromo-4-ethylthiolane

The compound with the maximum number of noncumulative double bonds is regarded as the parent compound of the monocyclic systems of a given ring size.

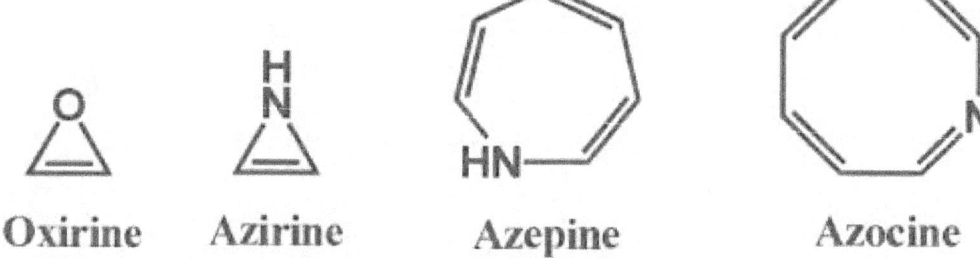

Oxirine   Azirine   Azepine   Azocine

Partial Unsaturation

Use fully unsaturated name with dihydro, tetrahydro, etc.

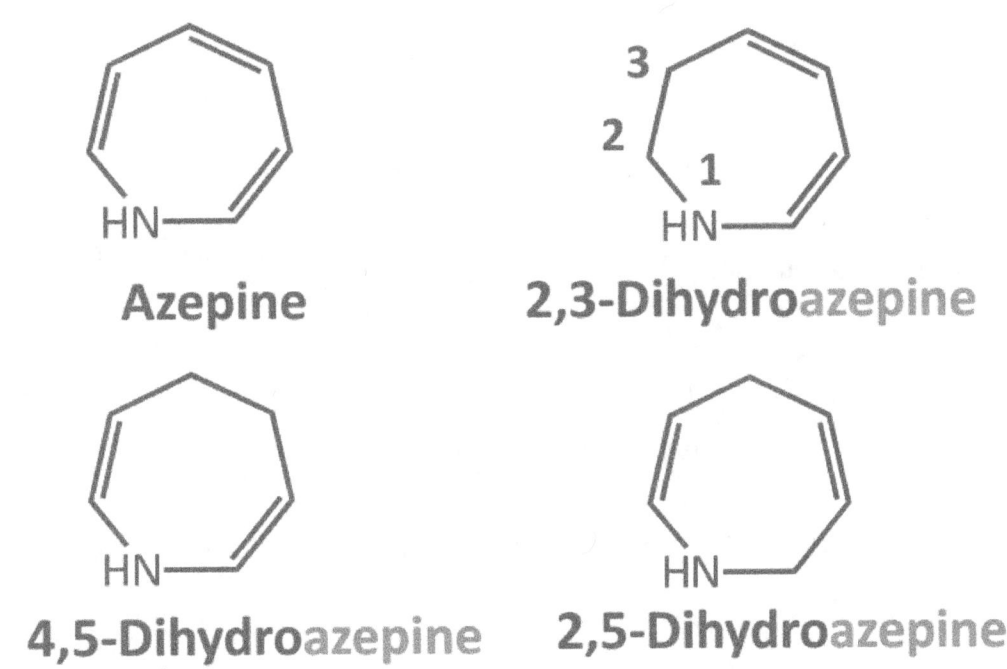

When numbering give priority to saturated atoms.

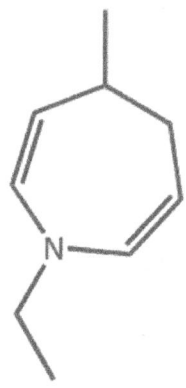

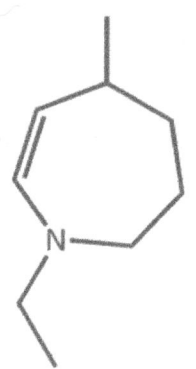

1-Ethyl-4-methyl-4,5-dihydroazepine

1-Ethyl-5-methyl-2,3,4,5-tetrahydroazepine

Rings With More Than One Heteroatom

Two or more similar atoms contained in a ring are indicated by the prefixes 'di-', 'tri', etc.

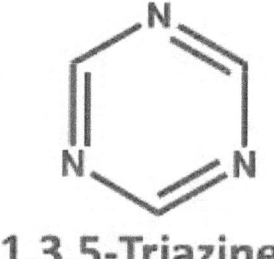

1,3,5-Triazine

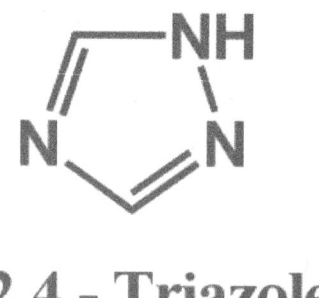

1,2,4 - Triazole

If more than one hetero atom occur in the ring then the heterocycle is named by combining the appropriate prefixes with the ending in Table I in order of their preference, O > S > N.

Oxaziridine

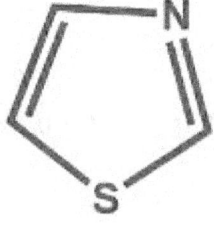

1,3-Thiazole
(Thiazole)

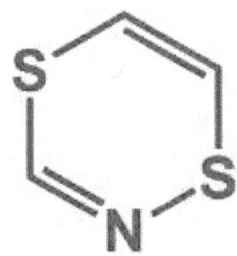

1,4,2 - Dithiazine

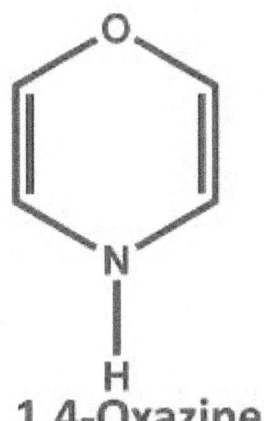

1,4-Oxazine

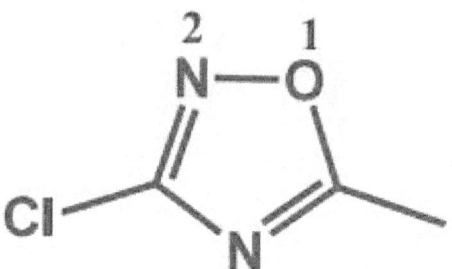

3-chloro-5-methyl-1,2,4-oxadiazole

Priority of heteroatoms for numbering purposes:

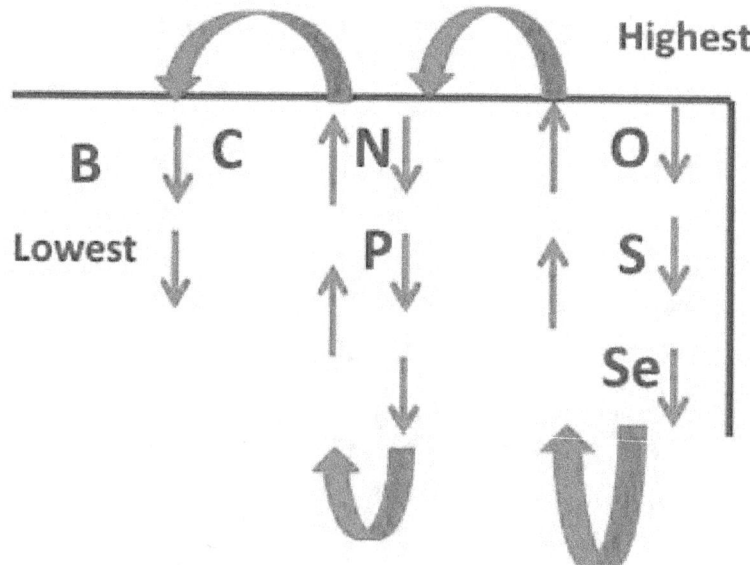

The ring is numbered from the atom of preference in such a way so as to give the smallest possible number to the other hetero atoms in the ring. As a result the position of the substituent plays no part in determining how the ring is numbered in such compounds.

4-Methyl-1,3-thiazole

II.   Common Names

There are a large number of important ring systems which are named widely known with their non-systematic or common names.

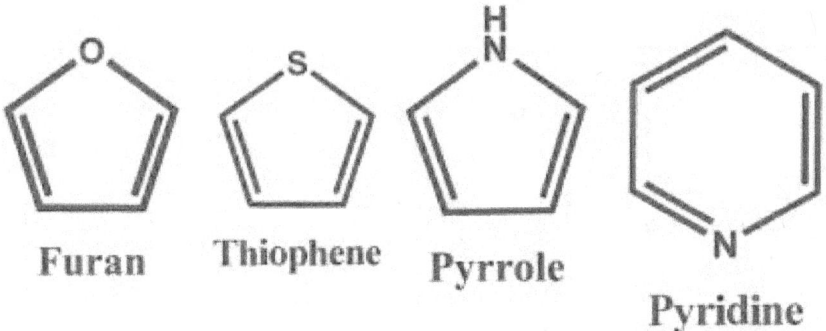

Furan   Thiophene   Pyrrole   Pyridine

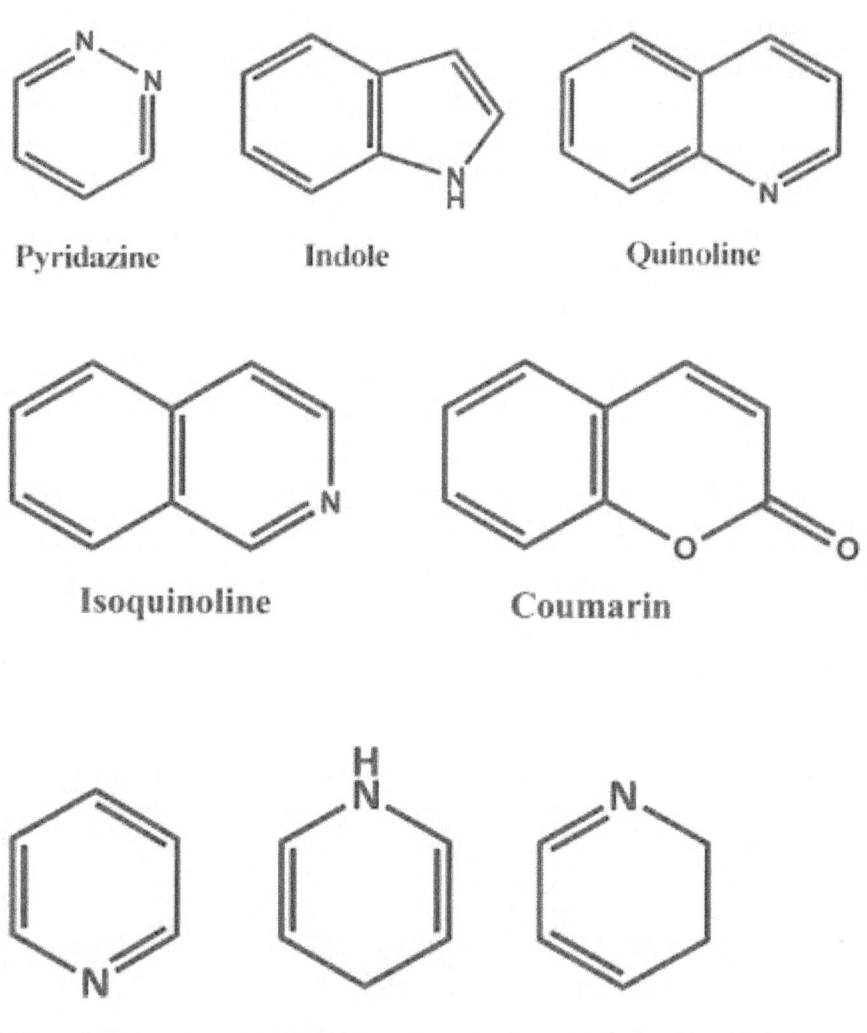

Pyridazine   Indole   Quinoline

Isoquinoline   Coumarin

Pyridine   1,4-Dihydropyridine   2,3-Dihydropyridine

Identical systems connected by a single bond

Such compounds are defined by the prefixes bi-, tert- , quater-, etc., according

to the number of systems, and the bonding is indicated as follows:

24

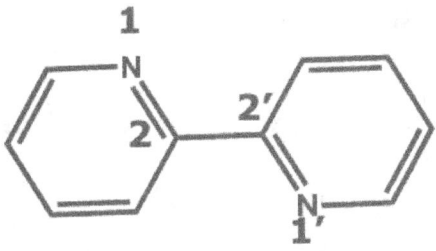

2,2' - Bipyridine

2,2': 4',3'' - Terthiophene

NAMING HETROCYCLES WITH FUSED RINGS

When naming such compounds the side of the heterocyclic ring is labeled by the letters a, b, c, etc., starting from the atom numbered 1. Therefore side 'a' being between atoms 1 and 2, side 'b' between atoms 2 and 3, and so on as shown below for pyridine.

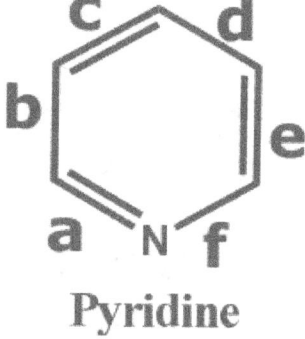

Pyridine

The name of the heterocyclic ring is chosen as the parent compound and the name of the fused ring is attached as a prefix. The prefix in such names has the ending 'o', i.e., benzo, naphtho and so on.

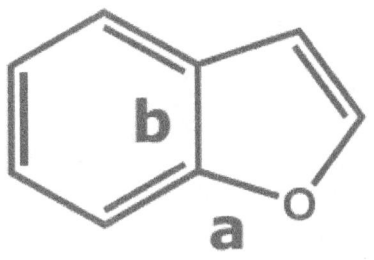

Benzo [b] furan

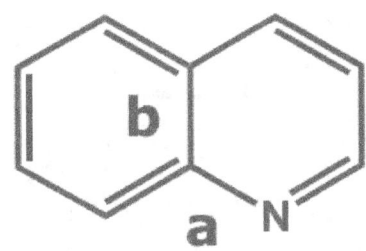

Benzo [b] pyridine

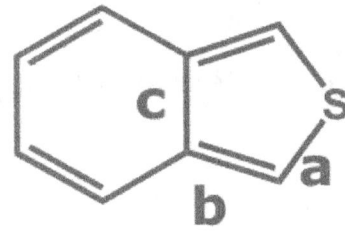

Benzo [c] thiophene

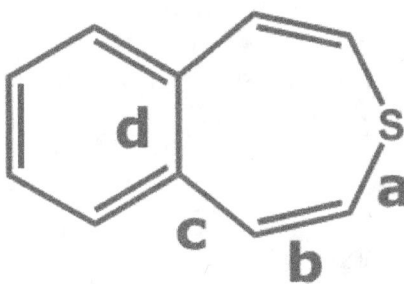

Benzo [d] thiepine

In a heterocyclic ring, other things being equal, numbering preferably commences at a saturated rather than at an unsaturated hetero atom.

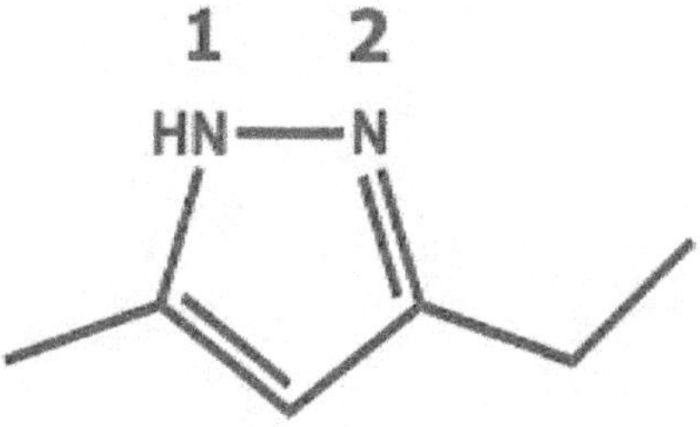

3-Ethyl-5-methylpyrazole 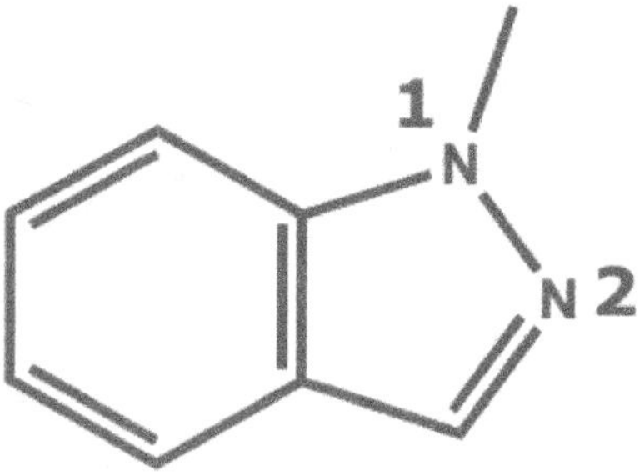   1-Methylindazole

HANDLING THE "EXTRA HYDROGEN"

Heterocycles with maximum number of double bonds which can be arranged in more than one way.

Examples

Pyrans

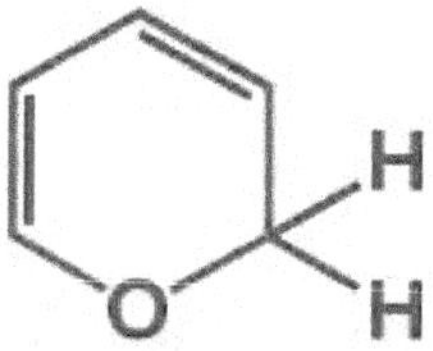

Double bonds
@ 2 and 4

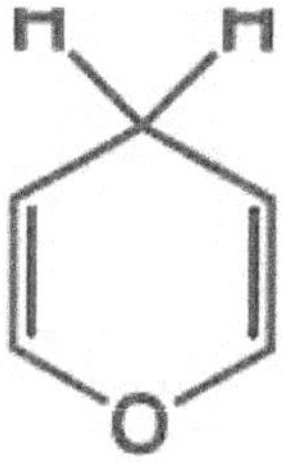

Double bonds
@ 2 and 5

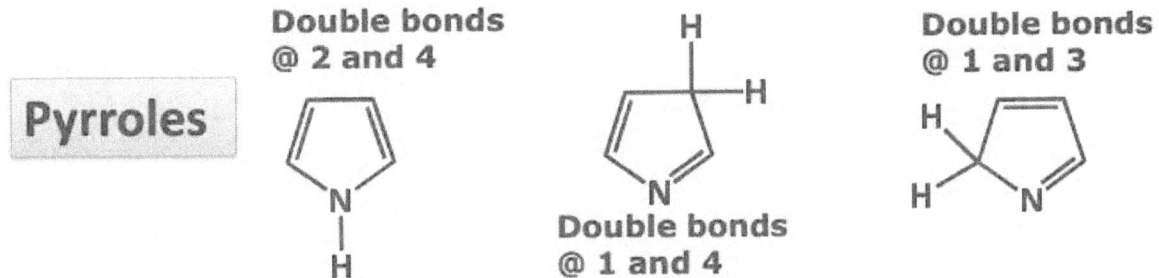

Pyrroles

Double bonds @ 2 and 4

Double bonds @ 1 and 4

Double bonds @ 1 and 3

Therefore, should have different names.

This is a special problem resulting from isomerism in the position of the double bonds which is sometimes referred to as "extra-hydrogen" and this can be addressed by simply adding a prefix that indicates the number of the ring atom that possesses the hydrogen using italic capital '1H' '2H' '3H', etc. The numerals indicate the position of these atoms having the extra hydrogen atom.

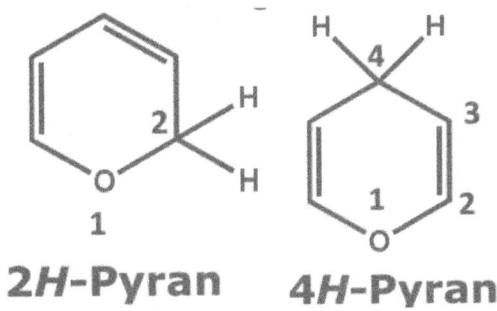

2*H*-Pyran   4*H*-Pyran

The saturated position takes priority in numbering.

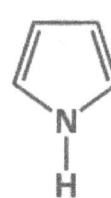

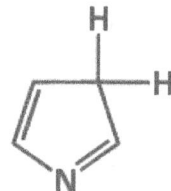

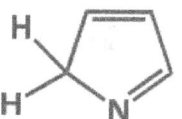

**1*H*-Pyrrole
(Pyrrole)**

3*H*-Pyrrole

2*H*-Pyrrole

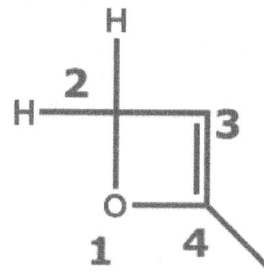

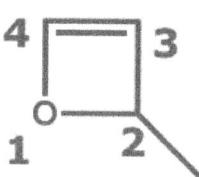

4-Methyl-*2H*-oxete

2-Methyl-*2H*-oxete

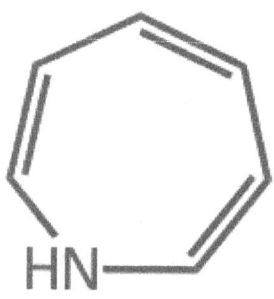

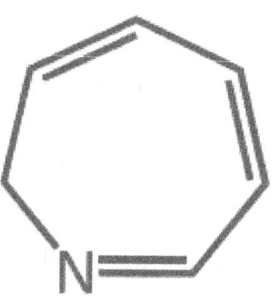

Azepine

2*H*-Azepine

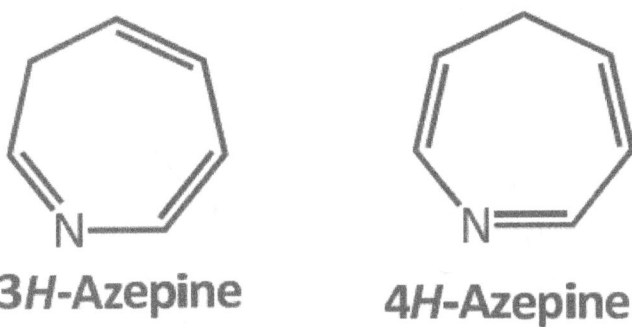

III. The Replacement Nomenclature

In replacement nomenclature, the heterocycle's name is composed of the carbocycle's name and a prefix that denotes the heteroatom. III. The Replacement Nomenclature Thus, "aza", "oxa", and "thia" are prefixes for a nitrogen ring atom, an oxygen ring atom, and a sulfur ring atom, respectively.

Heterocyclic rings are numbered so that the heteroatom has the lowest possible number.

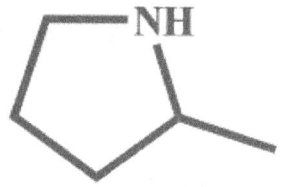

Azacyclopropane

or

Aziridine

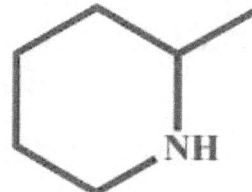

Azacyclobutane

or

Azetidine

2-Methylazolidine

or

2-Methylazacyclopentane

2-Methylazacyclohexane

or

2-Methylpiperidine

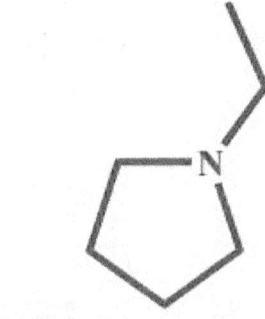

N-Ethylazacyclopentane
or
N-Ethylpyrrolidine

Oxacyclopropane
or
Oxirane
or
Ethyleneoxide

Oxacyclobutane
or
oxetane

**Oxacyclopentane
or
Tetrahydrofuran**

**Thiacyclopropane
or
Thiirane**

CHAPTER 3

FURANS: REACTIONS AND SYNTHESIS

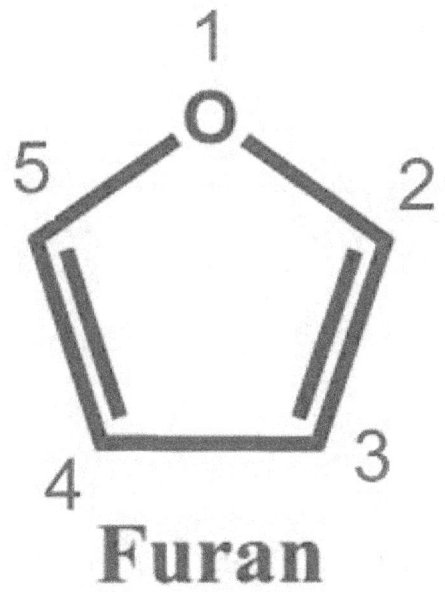

Furan

Furans are volatile, fairly stable compounds with pleasant odours. Furan itself is slightly soluble in water. It is readily available, and its commercial importance is mainly due to its role as the precursor of the very widely used solvent tetrahydrofuran (THF).

2.1 Reactions with Electrophilic Reagents

2.1.1 Substitution at Carbon

(i) Protonation

Furan and the simple alkyl - furans are relatively stable to aqueous mineral acids, though furan is instantly decomposed by concentrated sulfuric acid or by Lewis acids, such as aluminium chloride. Furan reacts only slowly with hydrogen chloride, either as the concentrated aqueous acid or in a non - hydroxylic organic solvent. Hot, dilute aqueous mineral acids cause hydrolytic ring opening.

α-protonated cation
which leads to α-exchange

β-protonated cation

+ H₂O   ring-opened products

O-protonated cation
present to minor extent

(ii) Reactions of Protonated Furans

The hydrolysis (or alcoholysis) of furans involves nucleophilic addition of water (or an alcohol) to an initially formed cation, giving rise to open - chain 1,4 - dicarbonyl - compounds or derivatives thereof.

Nitration

Reaction of furan, or substituted furans with acetyl nitrate produces non - aromatic adducts, in which progress to a substitution product has been interrupted by nucleophilic addition of acetate to the cationic intermediate, usually at C - 5. Aromatisation, by loss of acetic acid, to give the nitro - substitution product, will take place under solvolytic conditions, but is better effected by treatment with a weak base, like pyridine.   Further nitration of 2 - nitrofuran gives 2,5 - dinitrofuran as the main product.

Sulfonation

Furan and its simple alkyl - derivatives are decomposed by the usual strong acid reagents, but the pyridine – sulfur - trioxide complex can be used, disubstitution of furan occurring even at room temperature.

Halogenation

Furan reacts vigorously with chlorine and bromine at room temperature to give polyhalogenated products, but does not react at all with iodine.

Controlled conditions – bromine in dimethylformamide at room temperature – smoothly produce 2 - bromo - or 2,5 - dibromo - furans. The bromination probably proceeds via a 2,5 - dibromo - 2,5 - dihydro - adduct, indeed such species have been observed at low temperature using 1 H NMR spectroscopy.

If the bromination is conducted in an alcohol, trapping of the intermediate by C – 5 addition of the alcohol, then alcoholysis of C - 2 - bromide, produces 2,5 - dialkoxy - 2,5 - dihydrofurans, as mixtures of cis - and trans - isomers.

Acylation

Carboxylic acid anhydrides or halides normally require the presence of a Lewis acid (often boron trifl uoride) for Friedel – Crafts acylation of furans, though trifl uoroacetic anhydride will react alone. Aluminium - chloride - catalysed acetylation of furan proceeds faster at the α - position than at the β - position.

3 - Alkyl - furans substitute mainly at C - 2; 2,5 - dialkyl - furans can be acylated at a β - position, but generally with more difficulty. 3- Bromofuran is efficiently acetylated at C - 2 using aluminium chloride catalysis.

41

Alkylation

Mercuration

Mercuration takes place very readily with replacement of hydrogen, or carbon dioxide from an acid

Reactions with Oxidising Agents

Reactions with Nucleophilic Reagents

Simple furans do not react with nucleophiles by addition or by substitution. Nitro substituents activate the displacement of halogen, as in benzene chemistry, and VNS

methodology can also be applied to nitro - furans.

Metallation and Reactions of C -Metallated Furans

(i) Direct Ring C – H Metallation

Metallation with alkyllithiums proceeds selectively at an α - position,.

Metal – Halogen Exchange

Metallation at C - 3 can be achieved via metal – halogen exchange. The greater stability of a carbanion at an α - position shows up again in a mono - exchange of 2,3 - dibromofuran with selective replacement of the α - bromine.

Reactions with Reducing Agents

The best way to reduce a furan to a tetrahydrofuran is using Raney nickel catalysis, though ring opening, via hydrogenolysis of C – O bonds can be a complication.

Condensation with Imines and Iminium Ions

Mono - alkyl - furans undergo Mannich substitution under normal conditions.

45

Reaction scheme: 2-methylfuran + CH$_2$O, aq. Me$_2$NH / AcOH, 95 °C, 73% → 5-methyl-furfuryl-NMe$_2$

Reaction scheme: furan + [Me$_2$N=CH$_2$ Cl$^-$], (Me$_2$N)$_2$CH$_2$ / AcCl, MeCN, rt, 66% → furfuryl-NMe$_2$

Reaction scheme: furan-2-B(OH)$_2$ + Ph$_2$CHNH$_2$, HO$_2$CCH=O / CH$_2$Cl$_2$, H$_2$O, rt, 81% → product with NHCHPh$_2$ and CO$_2$H

Reaction scheme: furan + EtCHO, TolSO$_2$N=S=O / ZnCl$_2$, THF, rt, 73% → product with Et and NHTos

Electrocyclic Reactions

Furan also undergoes cycloadditions with allenes, with benzyne and with simpler dienophiles, like acrylonitrile and acrylate; various Lewis acidic catalysts can assist in some cases, zinc iodide is one such, hafnium tetrachloride another, and improved endo : exo ratios are obtained in an ionic liquid as reaction solvent.

46

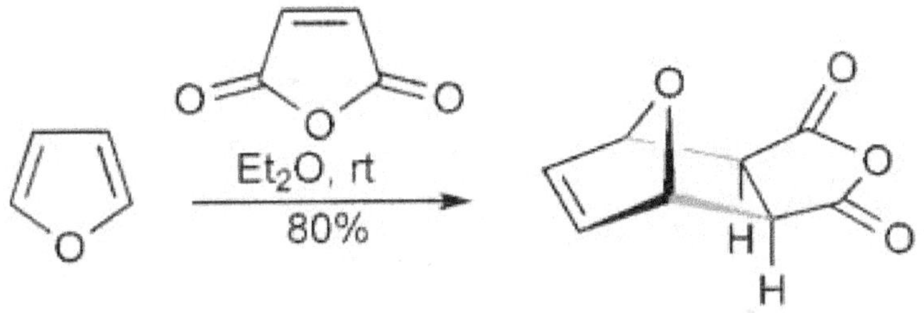
Et$_2$O, rt
80%
O
H
H

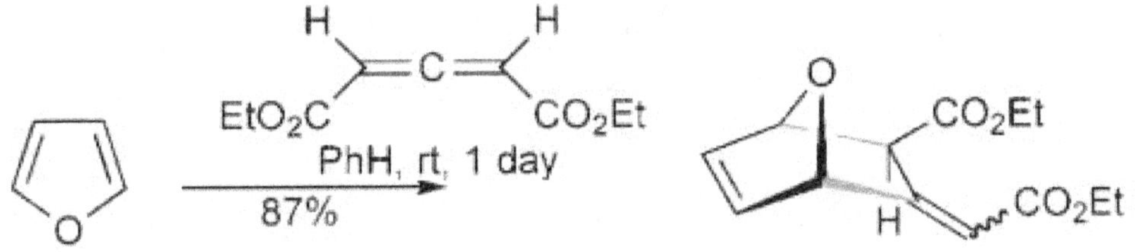
H
H
EtO$_2$C
CO$_2$Et
PhH, rt, 1 day
87%
O
CO$_2$Et
CO$_2$Et
H

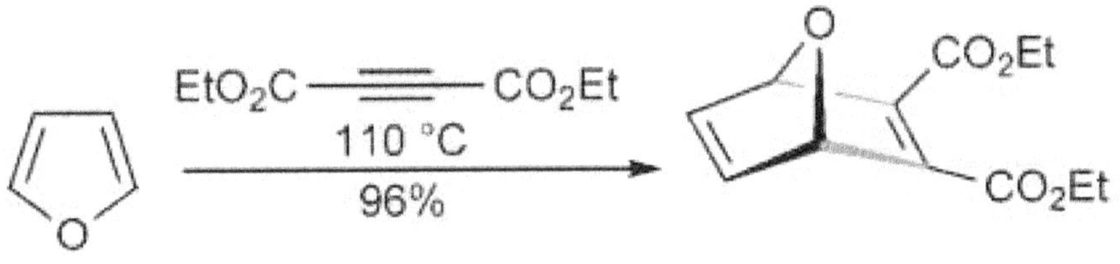
EtO$_2$C
CO$_2$Et
110 °C
96%
O
CO$_2$Et
CO$_2$Et

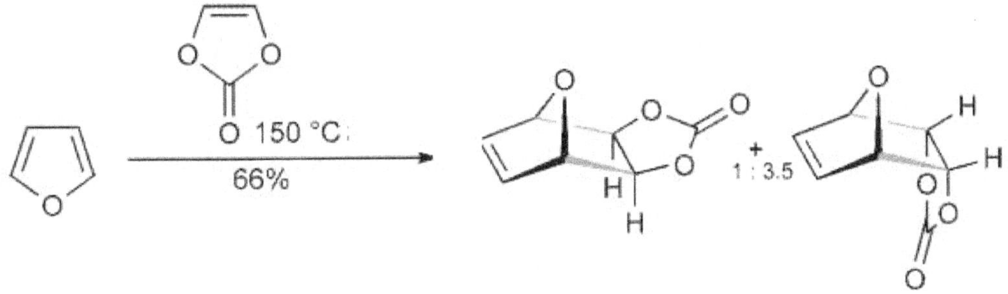
O
150 °C
66%
H
H
1 : 3.5

Photochemical Reactions

SYNTHESIS OF FURANS

The Paal – Knorr Synthesis

This involves heating of 1,4-dicarbonyl compounds in presence of P_2O_5

1,4-dicarbonyl compound
(R and R′ may be same or different.)

Furan

The Feist – Benary Synthesis

This is an organic reaction between α-halogen ketones and β-dicarbonyl compounds to substituted furan compounds. This condensation reaction is catalyzed by amines such as ammonia and pyridine. The first step in the ring synthesis is related to the Knoevenagel condensation. In the second step the enolate displaces an alkyl halogen in a nucleophilic aliphatic substitution.

R, R″ = Alk; R′ = Alk, OAlk

CHAPTER 4

PYRROLES: REACTIONS AND

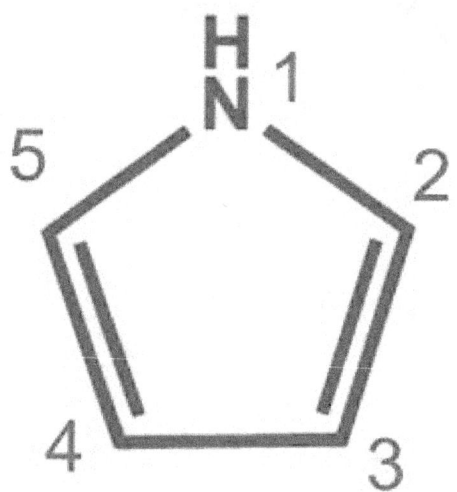

Pyrrole
1 H-pyrrole

4.1 Reactions with Electrophilic Reagents

Whereas pyrroles are resistant to nucleophilic addition and substitution, they are very susceptible to attack by electrophilic reagents and undergo easy C - substitution. Pyrrole itself, N - and C - monoalkyl - and to a lesser extent C , C ' - dialkyl - pyrroles, are polymerised by strong acids, so that many of the electrophilic reagents useful in benzene chemistry cannot be used. However, the presence of an electron – withdrawing substituent, such as an ester, prevents polymerisation and allows the use of the strongly acidic, nitrating and sulfonating agents.

Substitution at Carbon

Protonation

In solution, reversible proton addition occurs at all positions, being by far the fastest at the nitrogen, and about twice as fast at C - 2 as at C – 3

In the gas phase, mild acids like $C_4H_9^+$ and NH_4^+ protonate pyrrole only on carbon and with a larger proton affinity at C - 2 than at C – 3.

Thermodynamically, the stablest cation is the 2 H - pyrrolium ion, formed by protonation at C - 2 and observed p K aH values for pyrroles are for these 2 - protonated species. The weak N - basicity of pyrroles is the consequence of the absence of mesomeric delocalisation of charge in the 1 H - pyrrolium cation.

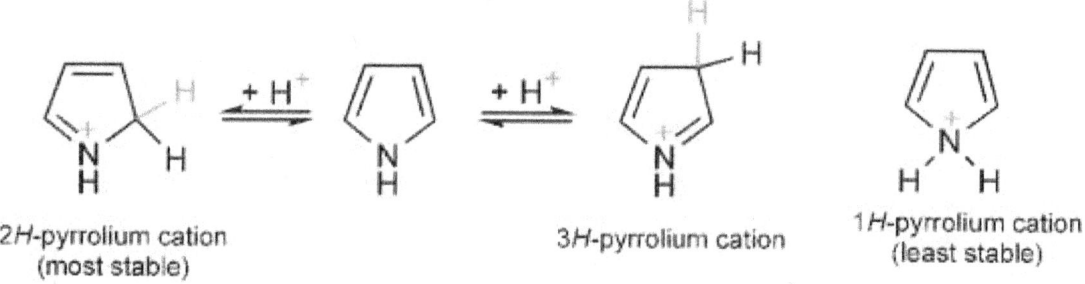

2H-pyrrolium cation
(most stable)

3H-pyrrolium cation

1H-pyrrolium cation
(least stable)

Reactions of Protonated Pyrroles

The 2 H - and 3 H - pyrrolium cations are essentially iminium ions and as such are electrophilic: they play the key role in polymerisation and reduction of pyrroles in acid. In the reaction of pyrroles with hydroxylamine hydrochloride, which produces ring - opened 1,4 - dioximes, it is probably the more reactive 3 H - pyrrolium cation that is the starter. Primary amines, RNH2 , can be protected, by conversion into 1-R- 2,5 - dimethylpyrroles, recovery of the amine being by way of this reaction with hydroxylamine.

Nitration

Nitrating mixtures suitable for benzenoid compounds cause complete decomposition of pyrrole, but reaction occurs smoothly with acetyl nitrate at low temperature, giving mainly 2 - nitropyrrole. This nitrating agent is formed by mixing fuming nitric acid with acetic anhydride to form acetyl nitrate and acetic acid, thus removing the strong mineral acid.

53

N - Substitution of pyrroles gives rise to increased proportions of β - nitration, even an N - methyl producing a β : α ratio of 1:3, and the much larger t - butyl actually reverses the relative positional reactivities, with a β : α ratio of 4:1. The intrinsic α - reactivity can be effectively completely blocked with a very large substituent such as a triisopropylsilyl (TIPS) group, especially useful since it can be subsequently easily removed.

Halogenation

Pyrrole reacts with halogens so readily that unless controlled conditions are used, tetrahalo - pyrroles are the only isolable products, and these are stable. Pyrrole reacts with halogens so readily that unless controlled conditions are used, tetrahalo - pyrroles are the only isolable products, and these are stable.

54

Acylation

Direct acetylation of pyrrole with acetic anhydride at 200 ° C leads to 2 - acetylpyrrole as main product, together with some 3 - acetylpyrrole, but no N - acetylpyrrole. N-Acetylpyrrole can be obtained in high yield by heating pyrrole with N- acetylimidazole. Alkyl substitution facilitates C - acylation, so that 2,3,4 -trimethylpyrrole yields the 5 - acetyl - derivative, even on refl uxing in acetic acid. The more reactive trifluoro acetic anhydride and trichloroacetyl chloride react with pyrrole effi ciently, even at room temperature, to give 2 - substituted products, alcoholysis or hydrolysis of which provides a clean route to pyrrole - 2 - esters or - acids.

Alkylation

Mono -   C - alkylation of pyrroles cannot be achieved by direct reaction with simple alkyl halides, either alone or with a Lewis - acid catalyst, for example pyrrole does not react with methyl iodide below 100 ° C; above about 150 ° C, a series of reactions occurs leading to a complex mixture made up mostly of polymeric material together with some poly - methylated pyrroles. The more reactive allyl bromide reacts with pyrrole at room temperature, but mixtures of mono - to tetra - allyl - pyrroles together with oligomers and polymers are obtained. Providing an appropriate acidic catalyst is chosen − one that will not cause polymerisation of pyrrole − reaction with alkenes carrying an electron - withdrawing group can be achieved.

Sulfonation

For sulfonation, a mild reagent of low acidity must be used: the pyridine – sulfur trioxide compound smoothly converts pyrrole into a sulfonate initially believed to be the 2 – isomer

Reactions with Oxidising Agents

Simple pyrroles are generally easily attacked by strong oxidising agents, frequently with complete break-down. Hydrogen peroxide is a more selective reagent and can convert pyrrole itself into a tautomeric mixture of pyrrolin - 2 - ones in good yield. Pyrroles which have a ketone or ester substituent are more resistant to ring degradation and high - yielding side - chain oxidation can be achieved using cerium(IV) ammonium nitrate, with selectivity for an α - alkyl.

Reactions with Nucleophilic Reagents

Pyrrole and its derivatives do not react with nucleophilic reagents by addition or by substitution, except in the same type of situation that allows nucleophilic substitution in benzene chemistry, i.e. where the leaving group is   ortho or   para to an electron - withdrawing group.

C - Metallation and Reactions of C - Metallated Pyrroles

Direct Ring C – H Metallation

The C - lithiation of pyrroles requires the absence of the acidic N - hydrogen, i.e. the

presence of an N - substituent, either alkyl or, if required, a removable group like phenylsulfonyl, carboxylate, trimethylsilylethoxymethyl, t - butylaminocarbonyl, diethoxymethyl or t - butoxycarbonyl. Even in the absence of chelation assistance to lithiation, metallation proceeds at the α - position.

SEMCl = $Me_3Si(CH_2)_2OCH_2Cl$

Metal – Halogen Exchange

Metal – halogen exchange on N - protected - pyrroles can provide access to either 2 - or 3 - lithio - pyrroles.

Reactions with Reducing Agents

Simple pyrroles are not reduced by hydride reducing agents or diborane, but are reduced

in acidic media, in which the species under attack is the protonated pyrrole.

Birch reduction of pyrrole carboxylic esters and tertiary amides gives dihydro -

derivatives; the presence of an electron - withdrawing group on the nitrogen serves both

to remove the acidic   N - hydrogen and also to reduce the electron density on the ring.

Electrocyclic Reactions (Ground State)

Simple pyrroles do not react as 4 π components in Diels – Alder cycloadditions: exposure of pyrrole to benzyne, for example, leads only to 2 - phenylpyrrole, in low yield. However N - substitution, particularly with an electron - withdrawing group, does allow such reactions to occur, Whereas pyrrole itself reacts with dimethyl acetylenedicarboxylate only by α - substitution.

Photochemical Reactions

The photo - catalysed rearrangement of 2 - to 3 - cyanopyrrole is considered to involve a 1,3 - shift in an initially formed bicyclic aziridine.

SYNTHESIS OF PYRROLES

Ring Synthesis

From 1,4 - Dicarbonyl Compounds and Ammonia or Primary Amines

1,4 - Dicarbonyl compounds react with ammonia or primary amines to give pyrroles

Paal – Knorr Synthesis

This reaction involves condensation of α–aminoketone with with a β-diketone or a β-ketoester to give substituted pyrrole.

α-amino ketone   R′ = -COR: β-diketone   Substituted pyrrole
R′ = -COOC₂H₅: β-ketoester

The van Leusen Synthesis

The stabilised anion of tosylmethyl isocyanide (TosMIC) (or of benzotriazol - 1 - ylmethyl isocyanide – BetMIC) adds in Michael fashion to unsaturated ketones and esters, with subsequent closure onto isocyanide carbon, generating the ring. Proton transfer, then elimination of toluenesulfi nate generates a 3 H - pyrrole that tautomerises to an aromatic pyrrole that is unsubstituted at both   α - positions.   Addition of the TosMIC anion to unsaturated nitro - compounds gives rise to 2,5 - unsubstituted - 3 - nitropyrroles.

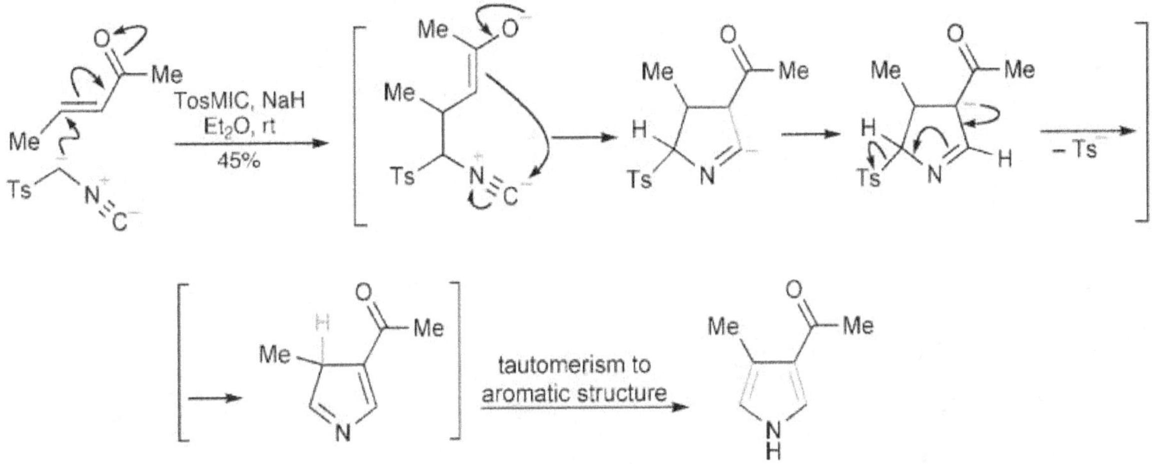

The Barton – Zard Synthesis

Formation of a pyrrole by condensation of a substituted nitroso-alkene with an isocyanoester:

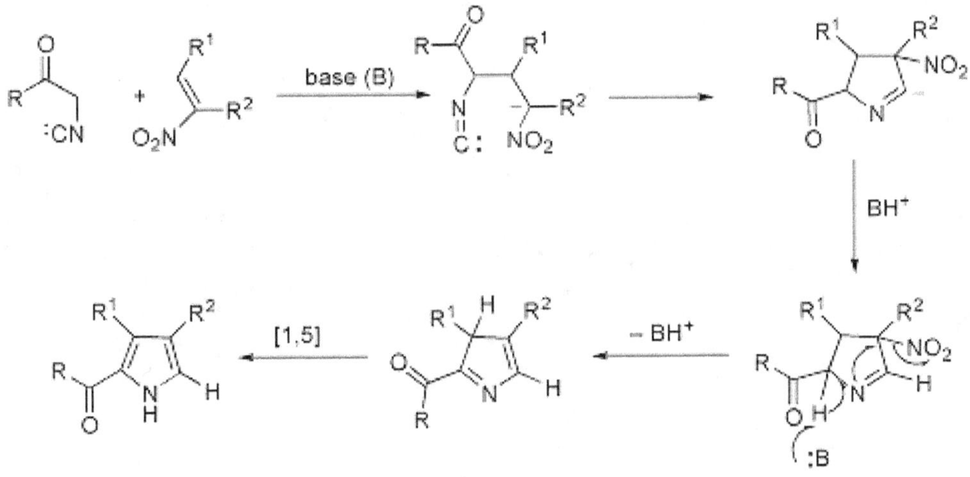

The Piloty – Robinson Synthesis

Formation of pyrroles by heating azines of enolizable ketones with acid catalysts, usually zinc chloride or hydrogen chloride:

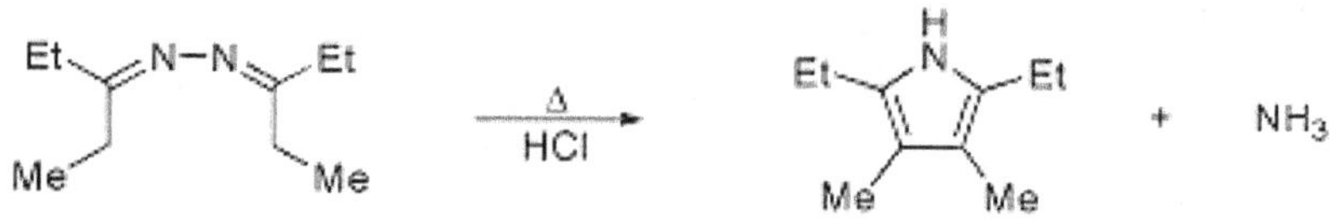

The Trofi mov Synthesis

This involves simply heating a ketoxime and acetylene in the presence of an alkali metal

hydroxide, generally in DMSO. The pyrrole products are 2,3 - unsubstituted. The process

is simple, though it does require handling acetylene at high temperature. Conditions are

available to produce either the pyrrole or, directly, an N - vinyl - pyrrole, complete with

a protecting group on nitrogen. The scheme suggests a probable mechanism.

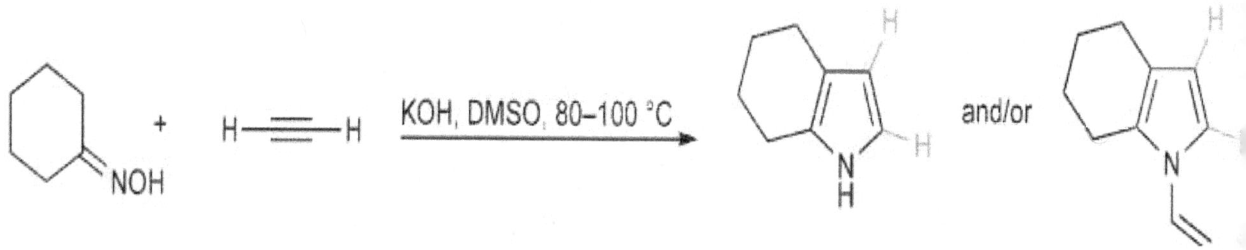

68

CHAPTER 5

THIOPHENE: REACTIONS AND SYNTHESIS

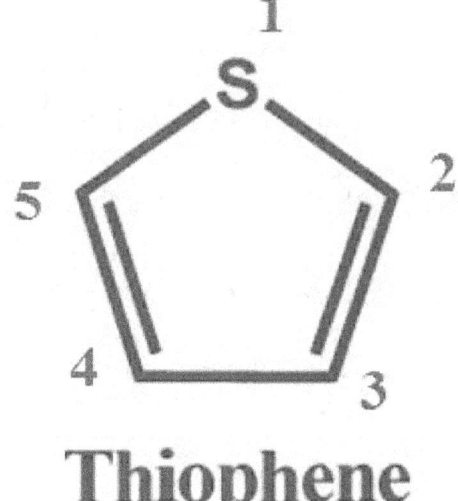

Thiophene

Reactions with Electrophilic Reagents

Substitution at Carbon

Protonation

Thiophene is stable to all but very strongly acidic conditions, so many reagent combinations that would lead to acid - catalysed decomposition or polymerisation of furans and pyrroles can be applied successfully to thiophenes.

Measurements of acid - catalysed exchange, or of protonolysis of other groups, for example silicon, or mercury, show the rate of proton attack at C - 2 to be about 1000 times faster than at C - 3.

Reactions of Protonated Thiophenes

The action of hot phosphoric acid on thiophene leads to a trimer; its structure suggests that, in contrast with pyrrole, the electrophile involved in the fi rst C – C bonding step is

the α - protonated cation.

Nitration

Nitration of thiophene needs to be conducted in the absence of nitrous acid, which can
lead to an explosive reaction.

2-Nitrothiophene

Sulfonation

Halogenation

Halogenation of thiophene occurs very readily at room temperature and is rapid even at -30 °C in the dark; tetrasubstitution occurs easily

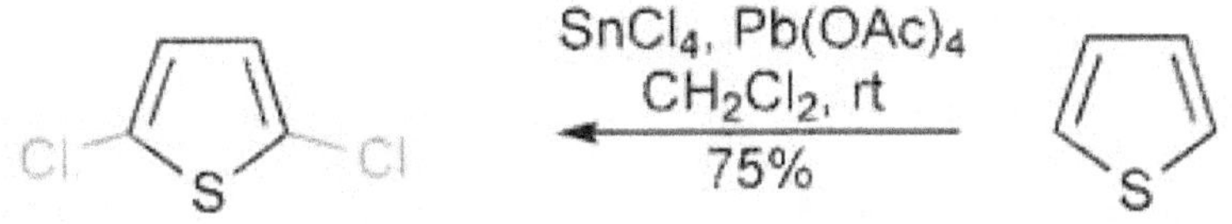
SnCl4, Pb(OAc)4
CH2Cl2, rt
75%
Cl
S
Cl
S

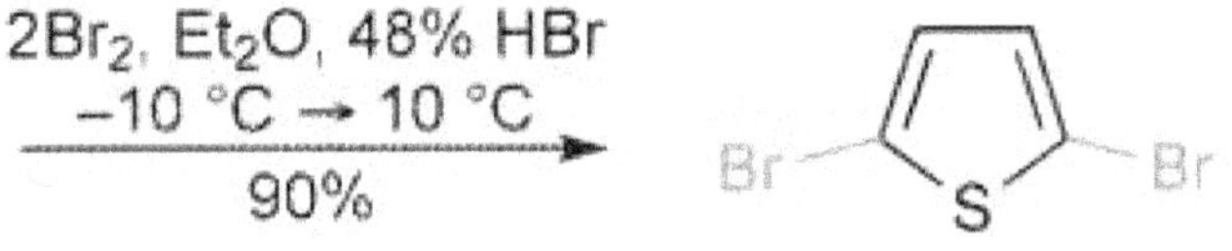
2Br2, Et2O, 48% HBr
−10 °C → 10 °C
90%
Br
S
Br

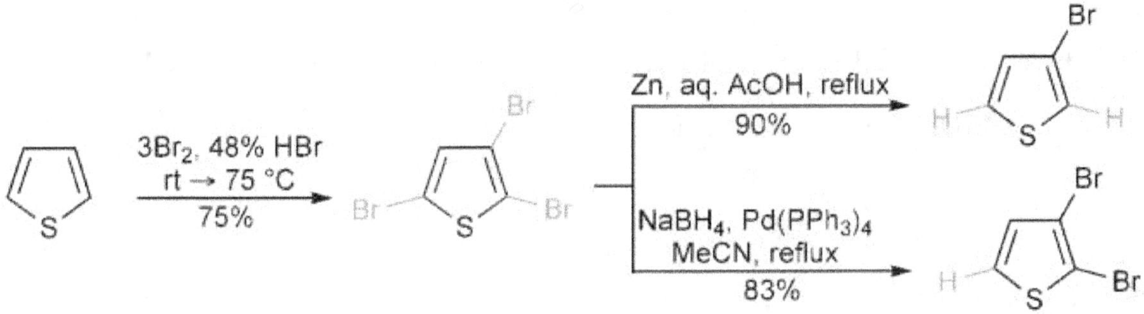
3Br2, 48% HBr
rt → 75 °C
75%
Zn, aq. AcOH, reflux
90%
NaBH4, Pd(PPh3)4
MeCN, reflux
83%
Br
H
S
S

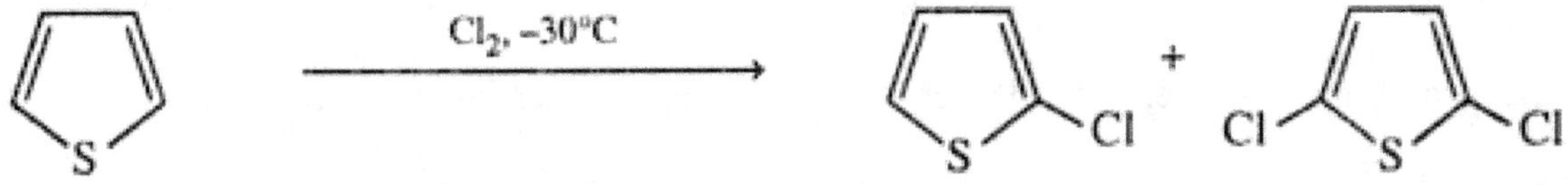
Cl2, −30°C
+
Cl
S

Thiophene 2-Chlorothiophene 2,5-Dichlorothiophene

Acylation

Alkylation

Alkylation occurs readily, but is rarely of preparative use, an exception being the efficient 2,5 - bis - t - butyl-ation of thiophene.

Mercuration

Thiophene reacts with Mercury (II) chloride in presence of sodium acetate to form corresponding 2- Mercury (II) chloride derivatives. Mercury group can be easily replaced by halogen and acyl group therefore this reaction is used as intermediate to prepare 2-substituted derivatives.

Reactions with Oxidising Agents

Apart from the S - oxidations discussed above, the thiophene ring system, unless carrying electron - releasing substituents, is relatively stable to oxidants; side - chains can be oxidised to carboxylic acid groups, though not usually in synthetically useful yields.

Reactions with Nucleophilic Reagents

Nitro substituents activate the displacement of leaving groups like halide.

Metallation and Reactions of C - Metallated Thiophenes

Direct Ring C – H Metallation

Monolithiation of thiophene takes place at C - 2; two mole equivalents of lithiating agent easily produces 2,5 - dilithiothiophene. 2 - Lithiated thiophene can be put to many uses, for example with N - tosylaziridine to introduce a 2 - tosylaminoethyl side - chain.

Metal – Halogen Exchange

Bromine and iodine at either α - or β - positions undergo exchange with alkyllithiums giving lithiated thiophenes. 2 - Bromo - and 2 - iodothiophenes readily form thienyl Grignard reagents. The reaction of 2,3 - dibromothiophene with n - butyllithium produces 3 - bromothien - 2 - yllithium.

Reactions with Reducing Agents

Sodium/ammonia treatment causes disruption of the ring in thiophene and simple thiophenes, however thiophene - 2 - carboxylic acid and 2 - acyl - thiophenes can be converted into the 2,5 - dihydro derivatives using lithium in ammonia, followed by protonation or trapping with an alkyl halide. Side - chain reductions can be carried out

with metal hydrides, which do not affect the ring. Simple saturation of the ring can be

achieved using ' ionic hydrogenation ' i.e. a combination of a trialkylsilane and acid,

usually trifl uoroacetic; the reduction proceeds   via a sequence of proton then ' hydride

'additions and consequently requires electron - releasing substituents to facilitate the first

step.

2,5 - Dihydro - products accompany tetrahydrothiophenes from reductions with zinc and
trifl uoroacetic acid.

Electrocyclic Reactions (Ground State)

 Unactivated thiophenes show little tendency to react as 4 π components in a Diels –

Alder sense; however, maleic anhydride   will react with thiophene to produce an adduct in high yield, under extreme conditions. Electrophilic alkynes will react with thiophenes under vigorous conditions, though the initial adduct extrudes sulfur, and substituted benzenes are obtained as products.

Thus, both   α -   and   β - methoxy - substituted thiophenes react with dimethyl acetylenedicarboxylate in xylene to give modest yields of phthalates resulting from sulfur extrusion from initial adducts; in acetic acid as solvent, only substitution products are obtained.

The strong tendency for thiophene   S,S - dioxides to undergo cycloaddition processes is echoed by thiophene   S - oxides. Thus, when thiophenes are oxidised with   meta - chloroperbenzoic acid and boron trifluoride (without which   S,S - dioxides are formed), in the presence of a dienophile, adducts from 2 + 4 addition can be isolated. Thiophenes that are 2,5 - or 3,4 - disubstituted with bulky groups can be converted into isolable   S -

oxides,   which undergo cycloadditions   syn to the oxide, as exemplified below.

Photochemical Reactions

The classic photochemical reaction involving thiophenes is the isomerisation of 2 - aryl -

thiophenes to 3 - aryl - thiophenes; the aromatic substituent remains attached to the same

carbon and the net effect involves interchange of C - 2 and C - 3, with C - 4 and C - 5

remaining in the same relative positions.

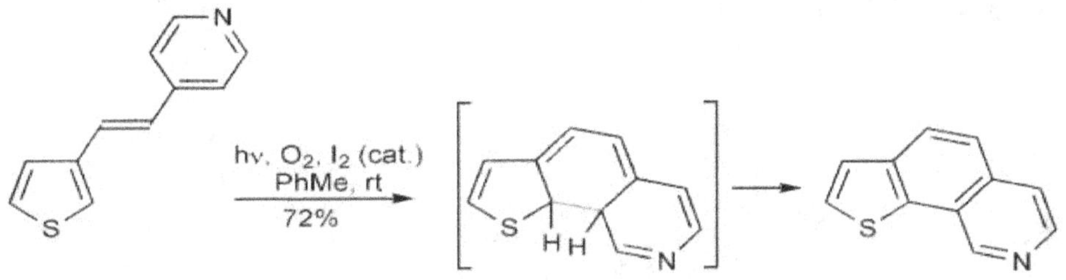

SYNTHESIS OF THIOPHENES

Ring Synthesis

From 1,4 - Dicarbonyl Compounds

Heating 1,4 - Dicarbonyl Compounds in presence of P_2S_3.

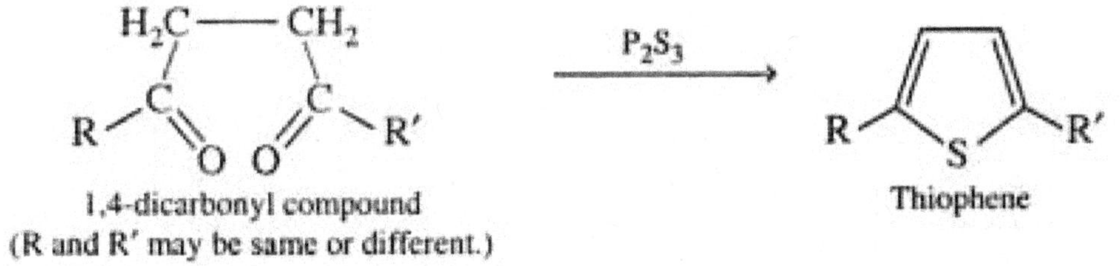

1,4-dicarbonyl compound
(R and R' may be same or different.)

Thiophene

The Hinsberg Synthesis

It describes the original condensation of diethyl thiodiglycolate and a-diketones under basic conditions which provides 3,4- disubstituted-thiophene-2,5-dicarboxylic acids

81

upon hydrolysis of the crude ester product with aqueous acid.

From Thio – Diketones

Thioglycolates react with 1,3 - dicarbonyl compounds (or equivalents) to give thiophene -

2 - carboxylic acid esters.

From α - Thio - Carbonyl Compounds

2 - Keto - thiols add to alkenyl - phosphonium ions, affording ylides, which then ring

close by Wittig reaction and give 2,5 - dihydrothiophenes, which can be dehydrogenated.

82

From Thiazoles

When thiazoles are heated strongly with an alkyne, generates 2,5 - unsubstituted thiophenes.

The Gewald Synthesis

The Gewald aminothiophene synthesis involves the condensation of aldehydes, ketones, or 1,3-dicarbonyl compounds 1 with activated nitriles such as malononitrile or cyanoacetic esters 2 and elemental sulfur in the presence of an amine to afford the corresponding 2-aminothiophene 3.

$R_1, R_2 = H$, alkyl, aryl, heteroaryl, CO_2R

$X = CN, CO_2R, COPh, CO$-heteroaryl, $CONH_2$

CHAPTER 6

PYRIDINES:
REACTIONS AND

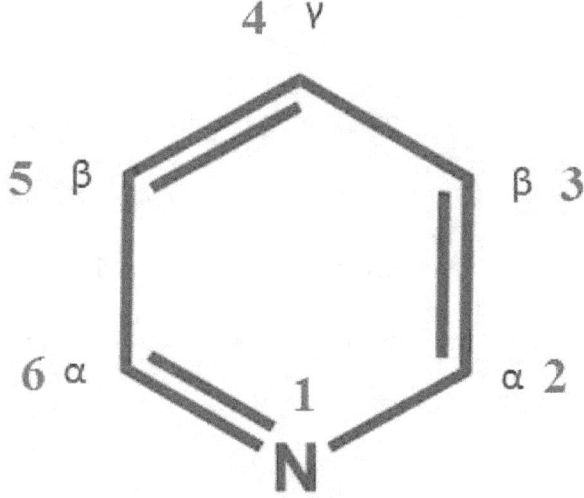

Pyridine

Reactions with Electrophilic Reagents

Addition to Nitrogen;

In reactions that involve bond formation using the lone pair of electrons on the ring nitrogen, such as protonation and quaternisation, pyridines behave just like tertiary aliphatic or aromatic amines. When a pyridine reacts as a base or a nucleophile it forms a ' pyridinium ' , cation in which the aromatic sextet is retained and the nitrogen acquires a formal positive charge

Protonation of Nitrogen

Pyridines form crystalline, frequently hygroscopic, salts with most protic acids. Electron - releasing substituents generally increase the basic strength. The basicities of pyridines carrying groups that can interact mesomerically as well as inductively vary in more complex ways, for example 2 - methoxypyridine is a weaker, but 4 - methoxypyridine a stronger base than pyridine; the effect of inductive withdrawal of electrons by the electronegative oxygen is felt more strongly when it is closer to the nitrogen, i.e. at C - 2.

Nitration at Nitrogen

This occurs readily by reaction of pyridines with nitronium salts, such as nitronium tetrafl uoroborate. Protic nitrating agents such as nitric acid lead exclusively to   N -

protonation.

Amination of Nitrogen

The introduction of nitrogen at a different oxidation level can be achieved with hydroxylamine   O - sulfonic acid   or using [N-   para - tolylsulfonylimino] phenyliodinane with copper(II) triflate;   the attacking species is nitrene.

Oxidation of Nitrogen

pyridines react smoothly with percarboxylic acids to give   N - oxides. There are many other ways to   N - oxidise pyridines: oxygen with ruthenium trichloride as catalyst is one example; hydrogen - peroxide – urea with trifl uoroacetic anhydride N - oxidises pyridines carrying electron - withdrawing groups. Similarly, there are many ways to deoxygenate pyridine N - oxides: samarium iodide, chromous chloride, stannous chloride with low - valent titanium, ammonium formate with palladium and catalytic hydrogenation all do the job at room temperature, molybdenum hexacarbonyl in hot ethanol is another alternative. The most frequently used methods have involved oxygen transfer to trivalent phosphorus or divalent sulfur. Ammonium formate with a palladium - on - carbon catalyst removes the oxygen and reduces the ring, smoothly giving piperidines.

pyridine *N*-oxide

Sulfonation at Nitrogen

Pyridine reacts with sulfur trioxide to give the crystalline, zwitterionic pyridinium - 1 - sulfonate, usually known as the pyridine sulfur trioxide complex. This compound is hydrolysed in hot water to sulfuric acid and pyridine.

When pyridine is treated with thionyl chloride, a synthetically useful dichloride salt is formed, which can, for example, be transformed into pyridine - 4 - sulfonic acid. The reaction is believed to involve initial attack by sulfur at nitrogen, followed by nucleophilic addition of a second pyridine at C – 4.

Halogenation at Nitrogen

Pyridines react easily with halogens and inter - halogens   to give crystalline compounds,

largely undissociated when dissolved in solvents such as carbon tetrachloride.

Acylation at Nitrogen

Carboxylic, and arylsulfonic acid halides react rapidly with pyridines generating 1 - acyl -

and 1 - arylsulfonyl - pyridinium salts in solution.

1-methylpyridinium
iodide

4-dimethylaminopyridine
(DMAP)

Alkylation at Nitrogen

Alkyl halides and sulfates react readily with pyridines at room temperature, giving quaternary N -substituted pyridinium salts. As with aliphatic tertiary amines, increasing substitution around the nitrogen, or around the halogen - bearing carbon, causes an increase in the alternative, competing, elimination process, which gives alkene and N - proto - pyridinium salt, thus 2,4,6 - trimethylpyridine (collidine) is used as a base in dehydrohalogenation reactions.

Substitution at Carbon

Electrophilic substitution of pyridines occurs very much less readily than for the correspondingly substituted benzene. The main reason is that the electrophilic reagent, or a proton in the reaction medium, adds fi rst to the pyridine nitrogen, generating a pyridinium cation, which is naturally very resistant to attack by an electrophile. When it does occur, electrophilic substitution at carbon must involve either highly unfavoured attack on a pyridinium cation or a relatively easier attack, but on a very low equilibrium concentration of uncharged free pyridine base.

Friedel – Crafts alkylation and acylation fail because pyridines form complexes with the Lewis - acid catalyst required, involving donation of the nitrogen lone pair to the metal centre. Milder electrophilic species, such as Mannich cations, diazonium ions or nitrous acid, which in any case require activated benzenes for success, naturally fail with pyridines.

Proton Exchange

H – D exchange via an electrophilic substitution process, such as will operate for benzene, does not take place with pyridine. A special mechanism allows selective exchange at the two α - positions in DCl – D$_2$O, or even in water at 200 °C, the key species being an ylide formed by 2/6 - deprotonation of the 1 H - pyridinium cation. Efficient exchange at all positions can be achieved at 110 °C in D$_2$O in the presence of hydrogen and palladium - on – carbon.

Nitration

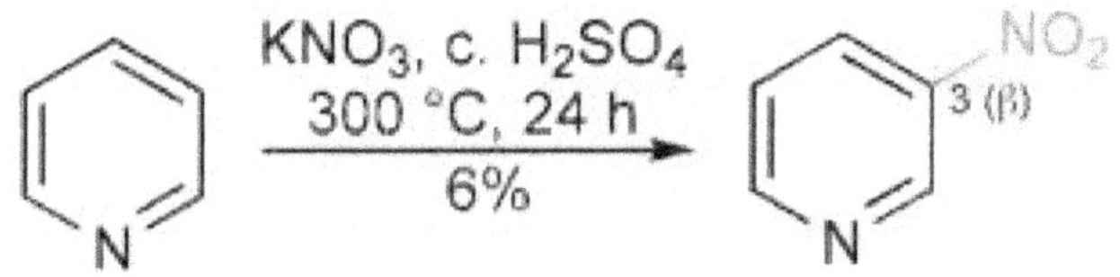

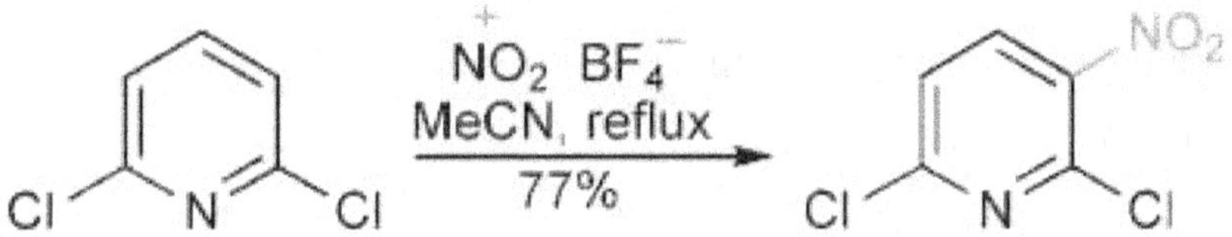

KNO$_3$, c. H$_2$SO$_4$
300 °C, 24 h
6%

NO$_2^+$ BF$_4^-$
MeCN, reflux
77%

Sulfonation

c. H$_2$SO$_4$
HgSO$_4$, 220 °C
70%

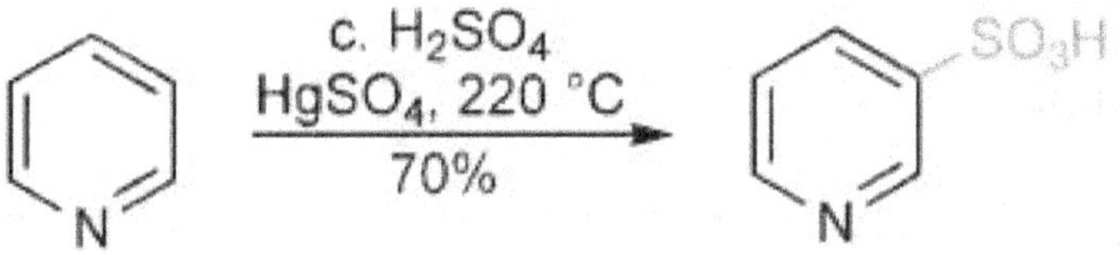

Halogenation

Cl$_2$
AlCl$_3$, 100 °C
33%

Br$_2$
66% oleum, 130 °C
86%

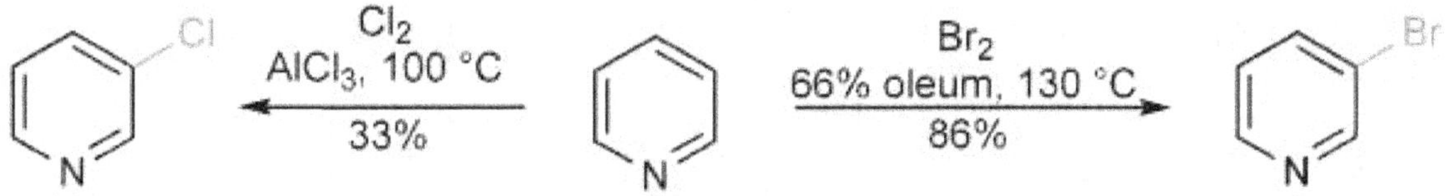

Actoxymercuration

The salt formed by the interaction of pyridine with mercuric acetate at room temperature can be rearranged to 3 - acetoxymercuripyridine by heating to only 180 ° C. This process, where again there is C - attack by a relatively weakly electrophilic reagent, like that described for mercuric - sulfate - catalysed sulfonation, may involve attack on an equilibrium concentration of free pyridine.

Reactions with Oxidising Agents

In acidic solution, pyridine is more resistant, but in alkaline media more rapidly oxidised, than benzene.

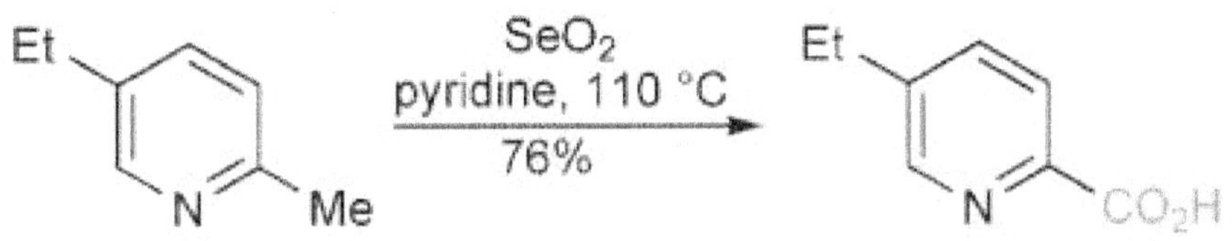

Reactions with Nucleophilic Reagents

Pyridine is a deactivated aromatic ring system. The elctron deficient position 2- and 4- are highly susceptible for nuleophilic attack.

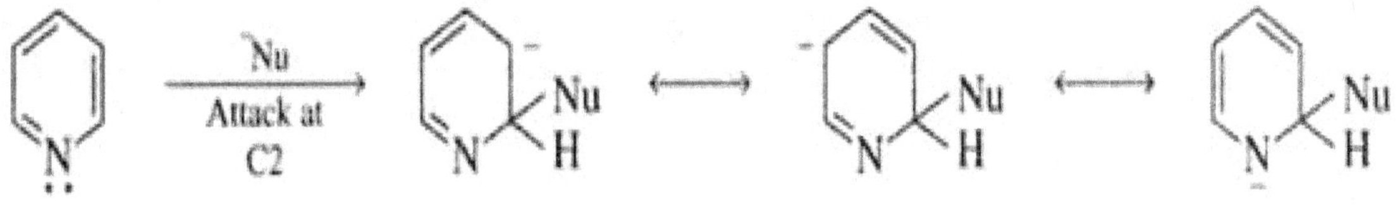

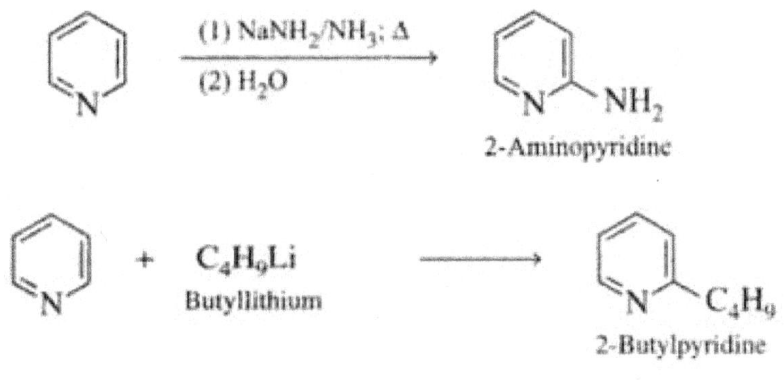

2-Aminopyridine

2-Butylpyridine

95

Phenyllithium → 2-Phenylpyridine

2-Hydroxypyridine ⇌ 2-Pyridone

Nucleophilic Substitution with 'Hydride' Transfer

Alkylation and Arylation

Reaction with alkyl - or aryl - lithiums proceeds in two discrete steps: addition to give a dihydro - pyridine   N - lithio - salt which can then be converted into the substituted aromatic pyridine by oxidation (e.g. by air), disproportionation or elimination of lithium hydride.

Amination

Amination of pyridines and related heterocycles, generally at a position   α   to the nitrogen, is called the Chichibabin reaction, the pyridine reacting with sodamide with the evolution of hydrogen. The ' hydride ' transfer and production of hydrogen probably involve interaction of amino - pyridine product, acting as an acid, with the anionic intermediate. The preference for   α- substitution may be associated with an intramolecular delivery of the nucleophile, perhaps guided by complexation of ring nitrogen with metal cation.

97

Silylation

pyridine is converted into 4 - trimethylsilylpyridine on reaction with trimethylsiliconide

anion.

Hydroxylation

Hydroxide ion, being a much weaker nucleophile than amide, attacks pyridine only at very high temperatures to produce a low yield of 2 – pyridine.

Metallation and Reactions of C - Metallated - Pyridines

Direct Ring C – H Metallation

When pyridine is heated to 165 ° C in MeONa – MeOD, H – D exchange occurs at all positions   via small concentrations of deprotonated species, at the relative rates   α : β : γ , 1 : 9.3 : 12.

Regioselective metallation at an   α - position of a pyridine can be achieved with the mixed base produced from two mole equivalents of   n - butyllithium with one of dimethylaminoethanol i.e. it is a 1   :   1 mixture of n - BuLi and Me $_2$N(CH $_2$) $_2$ OLi (BuLi - LiDMAE).

Metal – Halogen Exchange

Lithium derivatives are easily prepared by standard procedures and behave as typical organometallic nucleophiles, thus, for example, 3 - bromopyridine undergoes effi cient exchange with   n - butyllithium in ether at   − 78   ° C. With the more basic tetrahydrofuran as solvent, and at this temperature, the alkyllithium becomes more nucleophilic and only addition to the ring occurs, although the exchange can be carried

out in tetra-hydrofuran at lower temperatures.

Lithio - pyridines can also be prepared from bromo - pyridines at 0 ° C via exchange

using trimethylsilylmethyllithium (TMSCH 2 Li) and lithium dimethylaminoethoxide

(LiDMAE)

The combination of metal – halogen exchange with the presence of a directing substituent

can lead to regioselective metallation.

Dimerisation

Both sodium and nickel bring about ' oxidative ' dimerisations, the former giving 4,4 '

- bipyridine and the latter 2,2 ' - bipyridine. Each reaction is considered to involve the

same anion - radical resulting from transfer of an electron from metal to heterocycle, and

the species has been observed by ESR spectroscopy, when generated by single electron

transfer (SET) from lithium diisopropylamide.

Electrocyclic Reactions (Ground State)

There are no reports of thermal electrocyclic reactions involving simple pyridines. 2 -

Pyridones, however, participate as 4 π components in Diels – Alder additions, especially

under high pressure

Photochemical Reactions

SYNTHESIS OF PYRIDINES

Ring Synthesis

From 1,5 - Dicarbonyl Compounds and Ammonia

Ammonia reacts with 1,5 - dicarbonyl compounds to give 1,4 - dihydropyridines, which are easily dehydrogenated to pyridines. With unsaturated 1,5 - dicarbonyl compounds, or their equivalents (e.g. pyrylium ions),ammonia reacts to give pyridines directly.

From 1,3 - Dicarbonyl Compounds and 3-Amino-Enones or – Nitriles

Pyridines are formed from the interaction between a 1,3 - dicarbonyl compound and a 3 - amino - enone or 3 - amino - acrylate; 3 - cyano - 2 - pyridones result if cyanoacetamide is used instead of an amino - enone.

The Hantzsch Synthesis

This is a four-component reaction between an aldehyde, two equivalents of a β-ketoester and ammonia, followed by oxidation to give a pyridine-3,5-dicarboxylate. Subsequent decarboxylation gives the corresponding pyridines.

Dihydropyridine   Aromatic pyridine

Various stages of above reaction is:

Intermediate 1

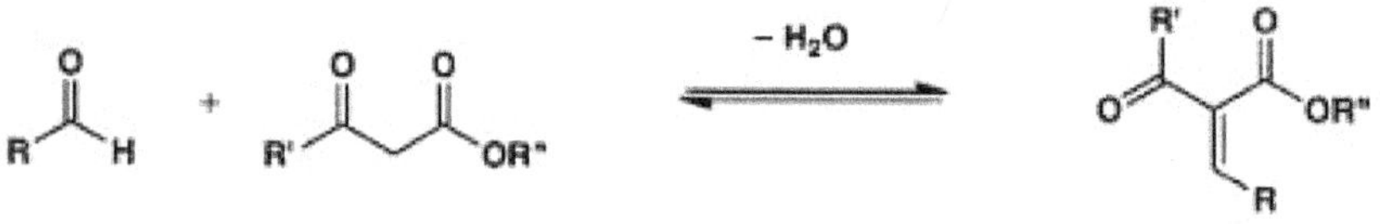

Intermediate 2

Intermediate 2

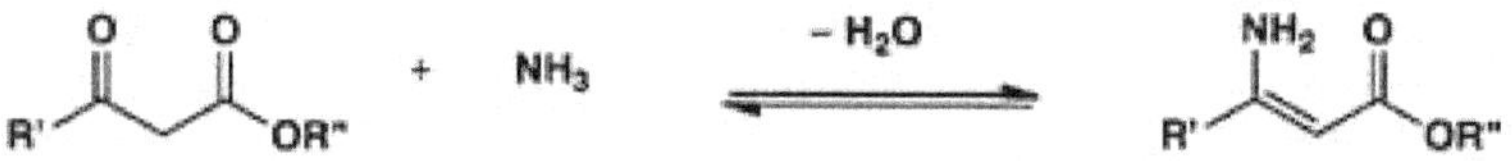

Oxidation

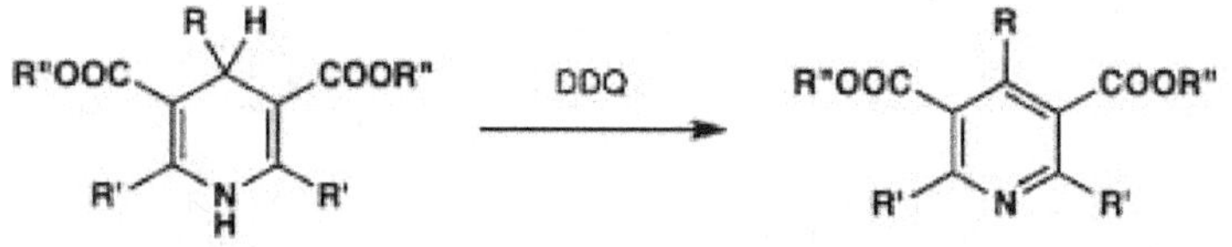

The Guareschi Synthesis

This reaction involves use of cyanoacetamide as the nitrogen - containing component and thus leads to 3 - cyano - 2 - pyridones. Providing the two carbonyl groups are sufficiently different in reactivity, only one of the two possible isomeric pyridine/pyridone products is formed via reaction of the more electrophilic carbonyl group with the central carbon of the 3 - amino - enone, 3 - amino - acrylate, or cyanoacetamide.

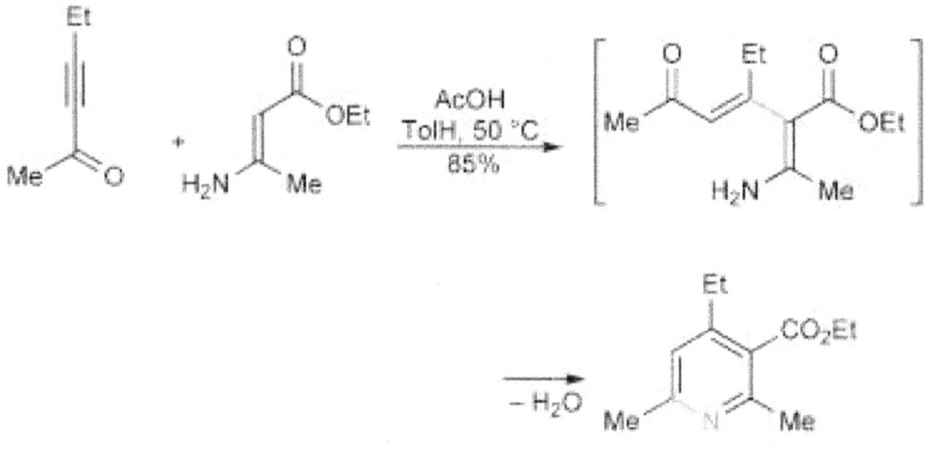

By Thermal Electrocyclisation of Aza - 1,3,5 – Trienes

Electrocyclisation of 1 - aza - 1,3,5 - trienes generates dihydropyridines, which can be oxidised to pyridines;however, if an oxime or hydrazine derivative is used, elimination of water or an amine in situ gives the pyridine directly. This method is particularly useful for fusion of pyridines to other ring systems and is illustrated by the example below:

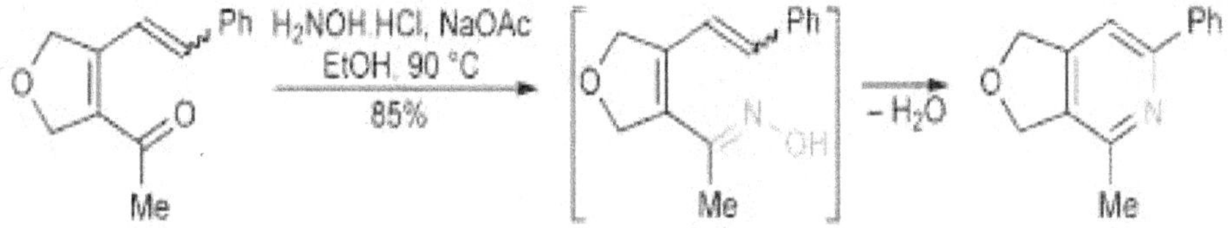

By Metal - Mediated [2 + 2 + 2] Cycloadditions

The cobalt - catalysed interaction of a nitrile and two equivalents of an acetylene (or one equivalent of each of two different acetylenes) brings three components together to form

an aromatic pyridine ring.

Cobalt has been used most often, in some cases on solid support,315 but the ring

construction can be brought about using a titanium(II) alkoxide, or with a nickel(0)

catalyst. Isocyanates with a ruthenium catalyst generate 2 – pyridines.

From Furans

Ring - opening and reclosure processes using furans include several signifi cant methods

for the construction of pyridines. 2,5 - Dihydro - 2,5 - dimethoxy - furans carrying as a C

- 2 side - chain an aminoalkyl group, give rise to 3 - hydroxy - pyridines.

From Enamides

Enamides, easily available by *N*- acylation of imines, can be converted into 2 - chloronicotinaldehydes by exposure to the Vilsmeier reagent: the example shows the putative intermediate.

110

CHAPTER 7

INDOLE: REACTIONS AND SYNTHESIS

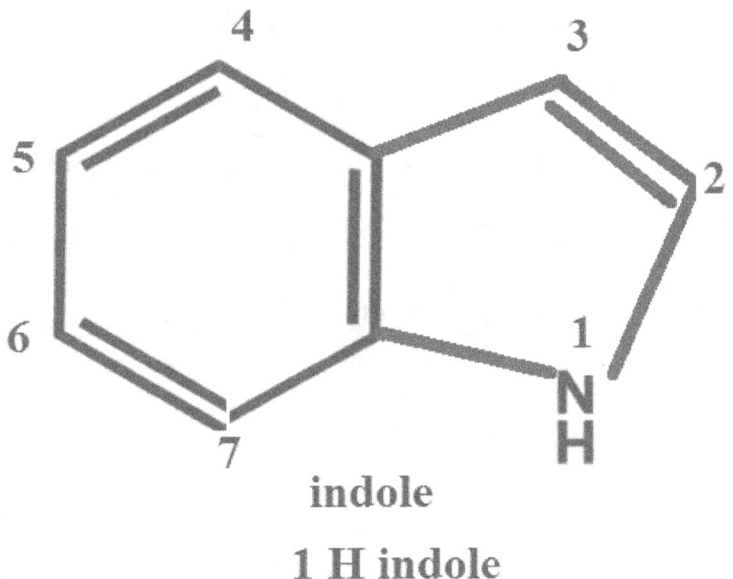

indole

1 H indole

Reactions with Electrophilic Reagents

Substitution at Carbon

Protonation

Indoles, like pyrroles, are very weak bases: typical pKaH values are: indole, − 3.5; 3 - methylindole, − 4.6; 2 - methylindole. − 0.3 This means, for example, that in 6M sulfuric acid, two molecules of indole are protonated for every one unprotonated, whereas 2 - methylindole is almost completely protonated under the same conditions. By NMR and UV examination, only the 3 - protonated cation (3 H - indolium cation) is detectable; it is the thermodynamically stablest cation, retaining full benzene aromaticity (in contrast to the 2 - protonated cation) with delocalisation of charge over the nitrogen and α - carbon. The spectroscopically undetectable N - protonated cation must be formed, and formed very rapidly, for acid - catalysed deuterium exchange at nitrogen is 400 times faster than at C - 3, 5 indeed the N - hydrogen exchanges rapidly even at pH 7, when no exchange at C - 3 occurs: clean conversion of indole into 3 - deuterioindole can be achieved by successive deuterio - acid then water treatments.

1*H*-indolium cation   2*H*-indolium cation   3*H*-indolium cation   2-methyl stabilises cation
(formed fastest)   (stablest)

That 2 - methylindole is a stronger base than indole can be understood on the basis of stabilisation of the cation by electron release from the methyl group; 3 - methylindole is a somewhat weaker base than indole.

Reactions of β - Protonated Indoles

Nitration;

Indole itself can be nitrated using benzoyl nitrate as a non - acidic nitrating agent; the usual mixed acid nitrating mixture leads to intractable products, probably because of acid - catalysed polymerisation. This can be avoided by carrying out the nitration using concentrated nitric acid and acetic anhydride at low temperature – under these conditions, N - alkylindoles, and indoles carrying electron - withdrawing N - substituents, but not indole itself, can be satisfactorily nitrated.

Mercuration

Indole reacts readily with mercuric acetate at room temperature to give a 1,3 - disubstituted product. Even N- sulfonyl - indoles are substituted under mild conditions; the 3 - mercurated compounds thus produced are useful in palladium - catalysed couplings and can be used to prepare boronic acids.

Thallation

Thallium trifl uoroacetate reacts rapidly with simple indoles, but well - defined products

cannot be isolated. 3 - Acyl - indoles, however, undergo a very selective substitution at C

- 4, due to chelation and protection of the heterocyclic ring by the electron - withdrawing

3 - substituent

Reactions with Oxidising Agents

Autoxidation occurs readily with alkyl - indoles, thus, for example, 2,3 - diethylindole gives an isolable 3 - hydroperoxy - 3 H - indole. Generally, such processes give more complex product mixtures resulting from further breakdown of the initial hydroperoxide; singlet oxygen also produces hydroperoxides, but by a different mechanism. If the indole carries a side - chain capable of trapping the indolenine by intramolecular nucleophilic addition, then tricyclic hydroperoxides can be isolated.

The reagent MoO 5 .HMPA, known as ' MoOPH ' , brings about addition of the elements of methyl hydrogen peroxide to an N - acyl - indole, and these adducts in turn, can be utilised: one application is to induce loss of methanol, and thus the overall transformation of an indole into an indoxyl

Oxidative cleavage of the indole 2,3 - double bond can be achieved with ozone, sodium periodate, potassium superoxide, with oxygen in the presence of cuprous chloride and

with oxygen, photochemically in ethanolic solution.

The conversion of 3 - substituted indoles into their corresponding oxindoles can be

brought about by reaction with dimethylsulfoxide in acid;

118

C - Metallation and Reactions of C - Metallated Indoles

Direct Ring C-H Metallation

C-Metallation of indoles has, in nearly all cases, been conducted in the absence of the much more acidic N - hydrogen i.e. the presence of an N - substituent like methyl, or if required, a removable group: phenyl-sulfonyl, lithium carboxylate and t - butoxycarbonyl have been used widely; also recommended are dialkylaminomethyl trimethylsilylethoxymethyl and methoxymethoxy.

Metal – Halogen Exchange

Reactions with Reducing AgentsThe indole ring system is not reduced by nucleophilic reducing agents, such as lithium aluminium hydride or sodium borohydride;

lithium/liquid ammonia does, however, reduce the benzene ring; 4,7 - dihydroindole is the

main product.

Reduction with lithium in the presence of trimethylsilyl chloride, followed by re-

aromatisation, produces 4 - trimethylsilylindole, an intermediate useful for the synthesis

of 4 - substituted indoles via electrophilic ipso - replacement of silicon.

$$\text{NaB(CN)H}_3$$
$$\underrightarrow{\text{AcOH, rt}}$$
$$94\%$$

$$\text{H}_2, \text{Pd(OH)}_2, \text{BaSO}_4$$
$$\underrightarrow{\text{AcOH, 60 °C}}$$
$$80\%$$

Electrocyclic and Photochemical Reactions

The heterocyclic double bond in simple indoles will take part in cycloaddition reactions

with dipolar 4 π components,   and with electron - defi cient dienes

$$\begin{array}{c} \text{MeHN} \quad \text{CO}_2\text{H} \\ (\text{CH}_2\text{O})_n, \text{TolH, reflux} \\ \hline 86\% \end{array}$$

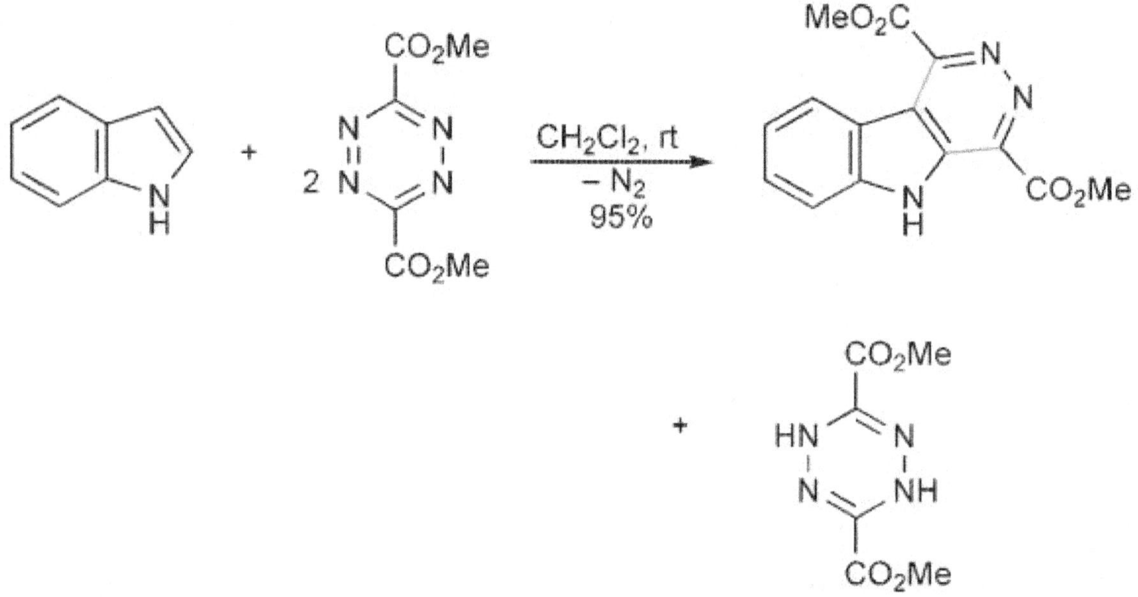

SYNTHESIS OF INDOLES

Ring Synthesis of Indoles

This involves heating an arylhydrazone, usually with acid, sometimes in an inert solvent gives an indole with the loss of ammonia.

The Fischer Synthesis

It involves the acid - or Lewis - acid - catalysed rearrangement of an arylhydrazone with the elimination of ammonia.

Mechanism

Application of Fischer Indole Synthesis

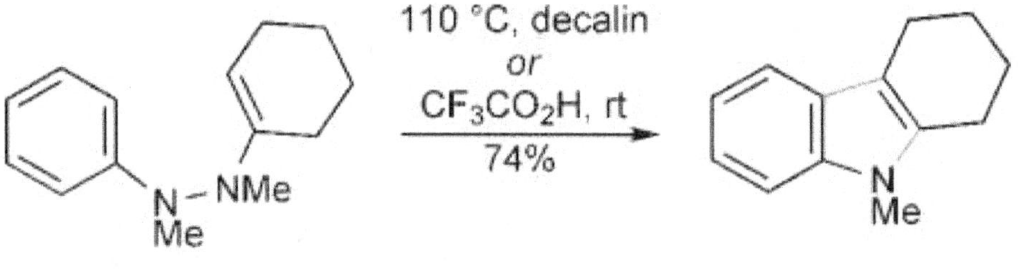
110 °C, decalin
or
CF3CO2H, rt
74%
N
Me
NMe
N
Me

2.

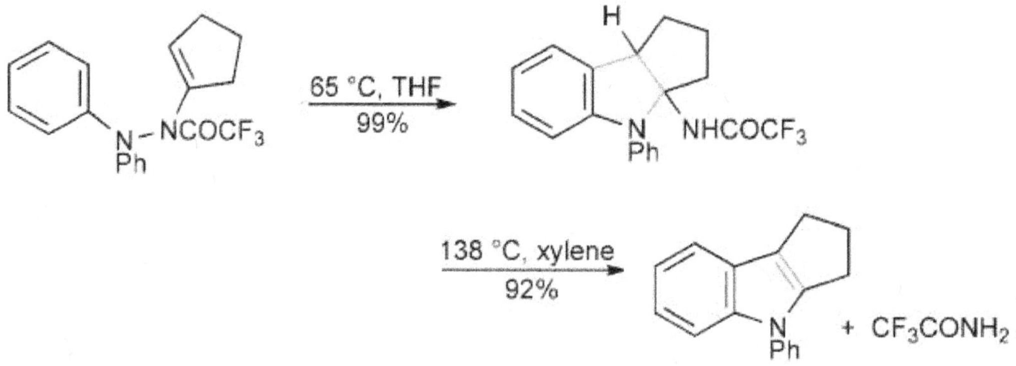
N
Ph
NCOCF3
65 °C, THF
99%
H
N
Ph
NHCOCF3
138 °C, xylene
92%
N
Ph
+ CF3CONH2

3.

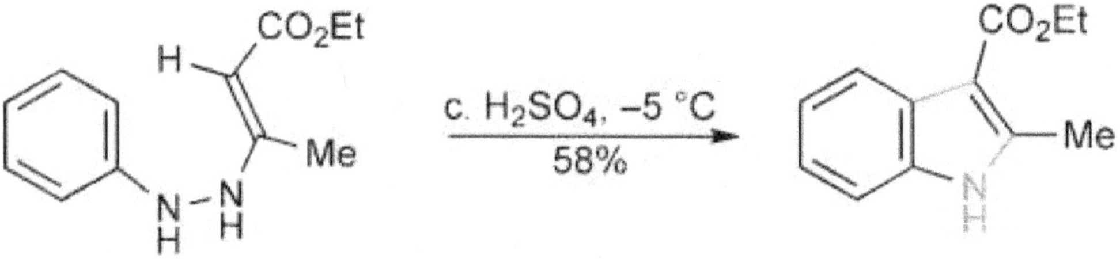
CO2Et
H
Me
N
H
N
H
c. H2SO4, –5 °C
58%
CO2Et
Me
NH

4.

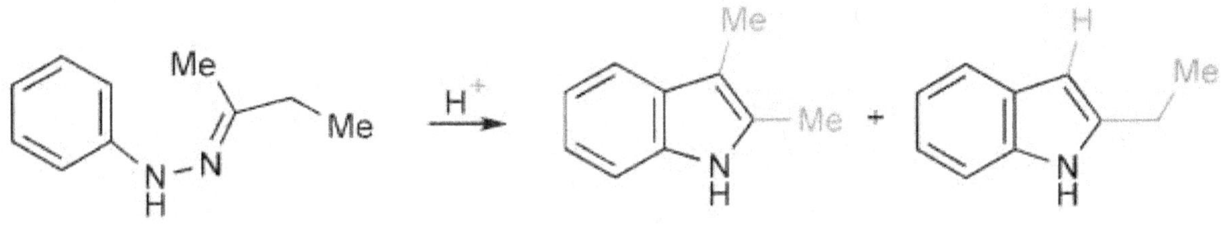
Me
Me
N
H
N
H+
Me
Me
N
H
H
Me
N
H

5.

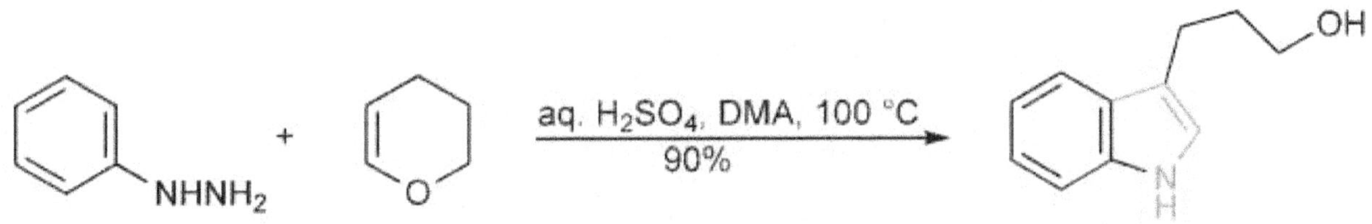
NHNH2
O
aq. H2SO4, DMA, 100 °C
90%
OH
N
H

6.

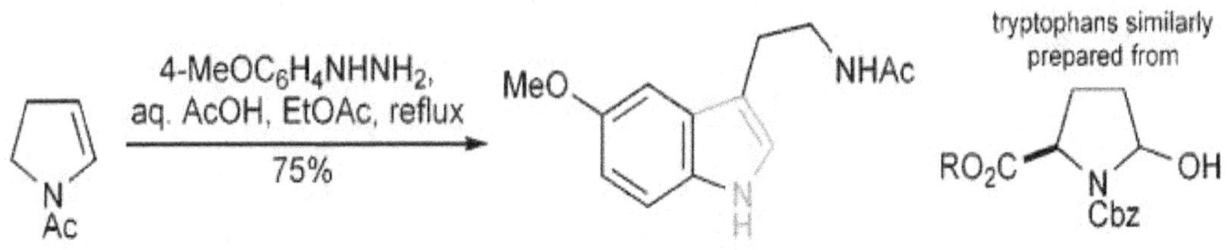
N
Ac
4-MeOC6H4NHNH2,
aq. AcOH, EtOAc, reflux
75%
MeO
NHAc
N
H
tryptophans similarly
prepared from
RO2C
N
Cbz
OH

7.

8.

The Grandberg Synthesis

The Reissert Synthesis

This is a series of chemical reactions designed to synthesize indole or substituted-indoles

(4 and 5) from ortho-nitrotoluene and diethyl oxalate

Leimgruber – Batcho Synthesis

This is a series of organic reactions that produce indoles from o-nitrotoluenes . The first step is the formation of an enamine 2 using N,N-dimethylformamide dimethyl acetal and pyrrolidine.[4] The desired indole 3 is then formed in a second step by reductive cyclisation.

Mechanism

The Madelung Synthesis

Mechanism

The Bischler Synthesis

This is a chemical reaction that forms a 2-aryl-indole from an α-bromo-acetophenone and excess aniline.

Mechanism

The first two step involve the reaction of the α-bromo-acetophenone with molecules of aniline to form intermediate **4**. The charged aniline forms a decent enough leaving group for an electrophilic cyclization to form intermediate **5**, which quickly aromatizes and tautomerizes to give the desired indole **7**.

Bartoli Synthesis

This is a reaction where a substituted nitroarene is converted to an indole using an excess of a vinyl Grignard reagent followed by an acid work-up. The substituents on the nitroarene affect the yield of this reaction where the highest yields are observed for ortho substituted reagents and the bulkier groups usually result in higher yields.

Mechanism

The Bartoli indole synthesis mechanism begins with a series of attacks on the nitroarene regent by the Grigrand reagents and is then followed by a 3,3 sigmatropic rearrangement (Claisen) step which results in an aldehyde intermediate. The aldehyde is then quickly attacked by the nearby nitrogen intramolecularly and a subsequent attack by the third equivalent of the Grignard reagent restored aromaticity. A final acid work-up step affords the indole product.

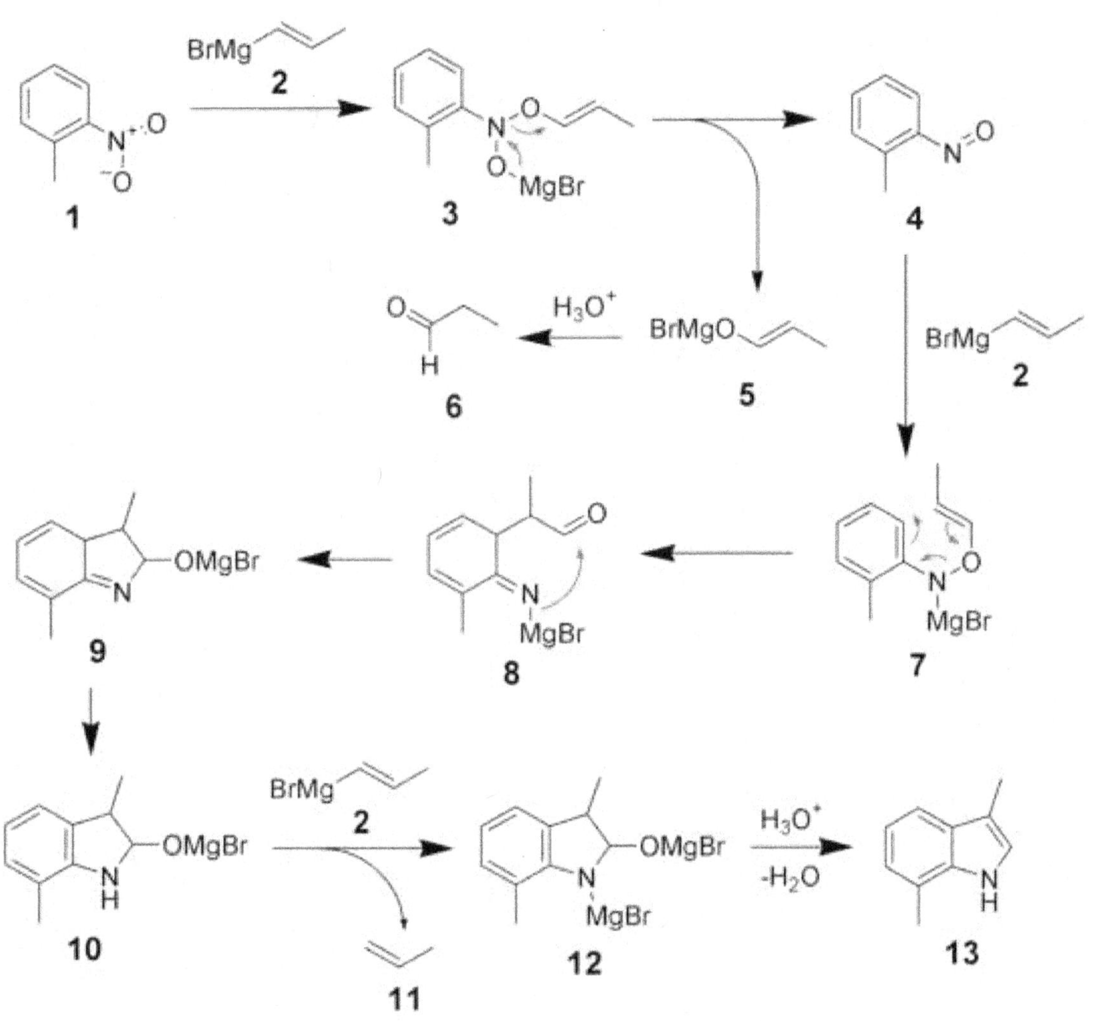
BrMg
2
1
3
4
5
6
7
8
9
10
11
12
13
MgBr
H3O+
BrMgO
OMgBr
-H2O

The Nenitzescu Synthesis

Mechanism

The Gassman Synthesis

This is a series of chemical reactions used to synthesize substituted indoles by addition of an aniline and a ketone bearing a thioether substituent.

Mechanism

The reaction mechanism of the Gassman indole synthesis is divided among three steps:-

The first step is the oxidation of the aniline 1 using tert-butyl hypochlorite (tBuOCl) to give the chloramine 2.

The second step is the addition of the keto-thioether to give the sulfonium ion 3, and is typically done at low temperatures (−78 °C).

The third and final step is the addition of a base, which in this case is triethylamine. Upon warming to room temperature, the base willdeprotonate the sulfonium ion creating the sulfonium ylide 4, which quickly undergoes a [2,3]-sigmatropic rearrangement to give

136

the ketone 5. The ketone 5 will undergo a facile condensation to give the desired 3-thiomethylindole 6.

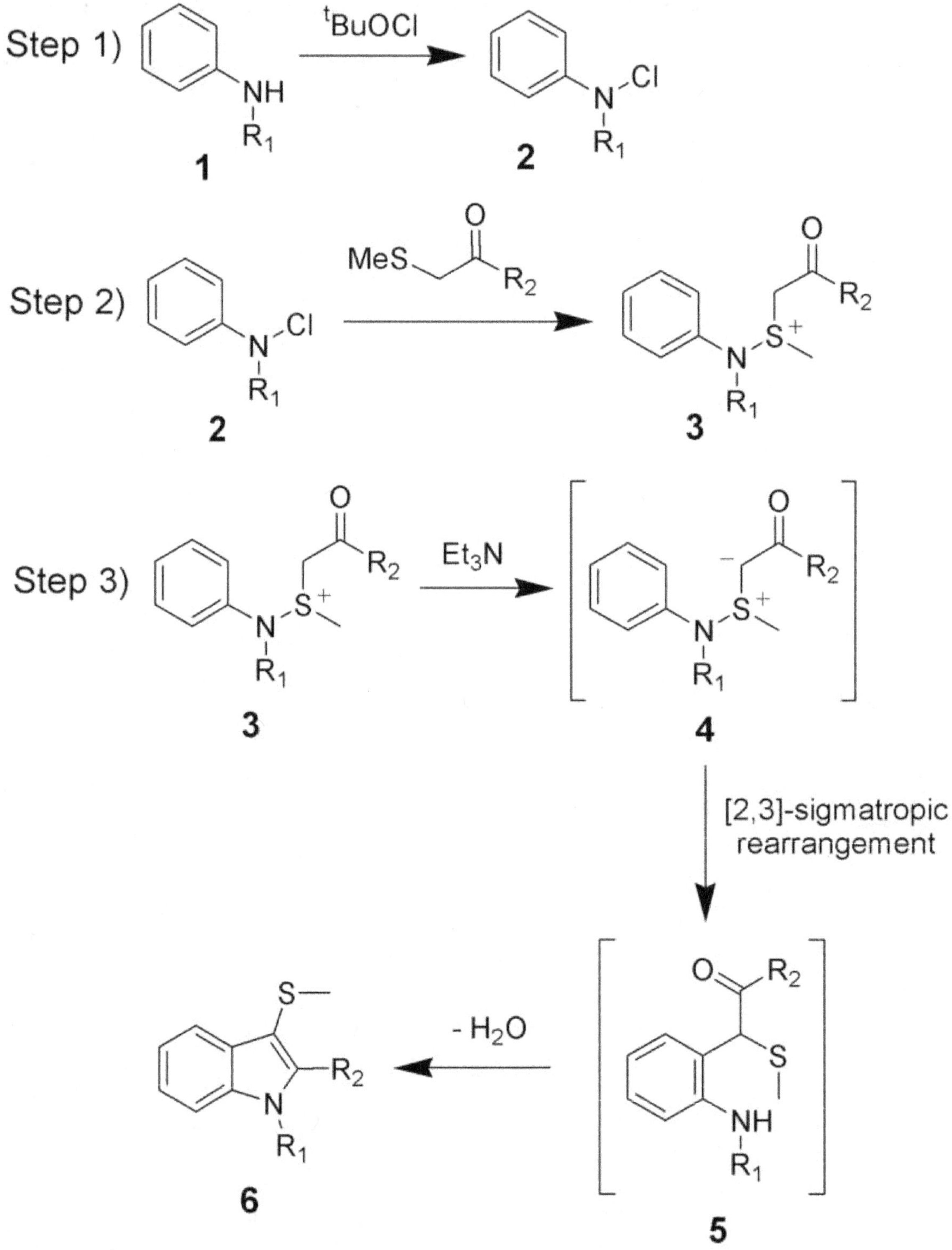

Step 1)
tBuOCl
NH
R1
1
N
Cl
R1
2
Step 2)
MeS
O
R2
3
Step 3)
Et3N
S+
4
[2,3]-sigmatropic rearrangement
5
- H2O
6

The Furstner Synthesis

This flexible synthesis depends on the reductive cyclisation of ortho - acyl - anilides with low - valent titanium – the conditions used for the McMurray coupling of ketones. In the example below, the cyclisation precursor was built up via the acylation of 2-tri-n - butylstannylthiazole

The Fukuyama Synthesis

Mechanism

CHAPTER 8

QUINOLINES AND ISOQUINOLINES: REACTIONS AND SYNTHESIS

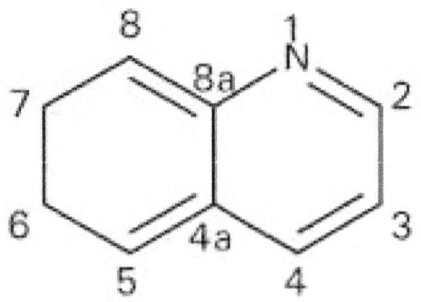

quinoline

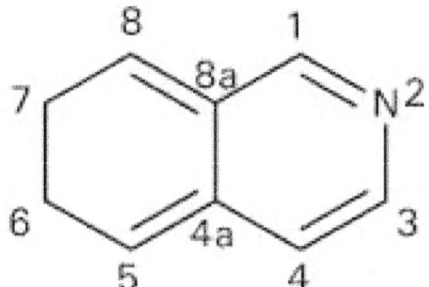

isoquinoline

Substitution at Carbon

Proton Exchange

Benzene ring C- protonation, and thence exchange, via N- protonated quinoline, requires strong sulfuric acid and occurs fastest at C-8, then at C- 5 and C- 6; comparable exchange in isoquinoline takes place somewhat faster at C- 5 than at C- 8. At lower acid strengths each system undergoes exchange α to nitrogen, at C-2 for quinoline and C - 1 for isoquinoline. These processes involve a zwitterion produced by deprotonation of the N-protonated heterocycle.

C-8 Exchange   C-2 Exchange

Nitration

The positional selectivity for proton exchange is partly mirrored in nitrations, quinoline gives approximately equal amounts of 5 - and 8 - nitro - quinolines, whereas isoquinoline produces almost exclusively the 5- nitro - isomer; mechanistically the substitutions involve nitronium ion attack on the N-protonated heterocycles.

Sulfonation

Sulfonation of quinoline gives largely the 8 - sulfonic acid, whereas isoquinoline affords the 5-acid. Reactions at higher temperatures produce other isomers, under thermodynamic control, for example both quinoline 8- sulfonic acid and quinoline 5 - sulfonic acid are isomerised to the 6 – acid.

Halogenation

Ring substitution of quinoline and isoquinoline by halogens is rather complex, products depending on the conditions used. In concentrated sulfuric acid, quinoline gives a mixture of 5 - and 8 - bromo derivatives; comparably, isoquinoline is efficiently converted into the 5-bromo - derivative in the presence of aluminium chloride, or with N- bromosuccinimide in concentrated sulfuric acid. Introduction of halogen to the hetero - rings occurs under remarkably mild conditions in which halide addition to a salt initiates the sequence. Thus treatment of quinoline or isoquinoline hydrochlorides with bromine produces 3-bromoquinoline and 4 - bromoisoquinoline, respectively.

Reactions with Nucleophilic Reagents

Nucleophilic Substitution with ' Hydride ' Transfer

Reactions of this type occur fastest at C - 2 in quinoline and at C - 1 in isoquinolines

Alkylation and Arylation

The immediate products of addition of alkyl and aryl Grignard reagents and alkyl – and

aryllithiums are dihydro - quinolines and - isoquinolines and can be characterised as such,

but can be oxidised to afford the C- substituted, re- aromatised heterocycles; illustrated

below is a 2 - arylation of quinoline.

Amination and Nitration

Sodium amide reacts rapidly and completely with quinoline and isoquinoline, even at −45° C, to givedihydro - adducts with initial amide attack at C - 2 (main) and C - 4(minor) in quinoline, and C - 1 in isoquinoline.

Hydroxylation

Both quinoline and isoquinoline can be directly hydroxylated with potassium hydroxide at high temperature with the evolution of hydrogen. 2 - Quinolone and 1 - isoquinolone are the isolated products.

Metallation and Reactions of *C*- Metallated Quinolines and Isoquinolines

Direct Ring C–H Metallation

Direct lithiation, i.e. *C*- deprotonation of quinolines31 requires an adjacent substituent, such as chlorine, fluorine or alkoxy.

148

Metal – Halogen Exchange

Reactions with Reducing Agents

Selective reduction of either the pyridine or the benzene rings in quinoline and isoquinoline can be achieved: the heterocyclic ring is reduced to the tetrahydro level by sodium cyanoborohydride in acid solution, bysodium borohydride in the presence of nickel(II) chloride,by zinc borohydride or, traditionally, by room temperature and room pressure catalytic hydrogenation in methanol. In strong acid solution it is the benzene ring which is selectively saturated; longer reaction times can then lead to decahydro derivatives. Treatment of quinoline and isoquinoline with sodium borohydride in a mixture of acetic acid and acetic anhydride gives good yields of *N*- acetyl - 1,2 - dihydro derivatives.

Lithium in liquid ammonia conditions can produce 1,4 - dihydroquinoline47 and 3,4-dihydroisoquinoline.Conversely, lithium aluminium hydride reduces generating 1,2 - dihydroquinoline and 1,2 - dihydroisoquinoline. These dihydro - heterocycles can be easily oxidised back to the fully aromatic systems, or disproportionate, especially in acid solution, to give a mixture of tetrahydro and re – aromatized compounds.

SYNTHESIS OF QUINOLINES AND ISOQUINOLINES

Quinolines from Aryl - Amines and 1,3 - Dicarbonyl Compounds

Anilines react with 1,3 - dicarbonyl compounds to give intermediates which can be cyclised with acid.

The Combes Synthesis

Condensation of a 1,3 - dicarbonyl compound with an arylamine gives a high yield of a β-amino - enone, which can then be cyclised with concentrated acid.100 Mechanistically, the cyclisation step is an electrophilic substitution by the O- protonated amino- enone, followed by loss of water to give the aromatic quinoline.

Conrad – Limpach – Knorr Reaction

If the 1,3 - dicarbonyl component is at the 1,3 - keto acid oxidation level, then the product is a quinolone. Anilines and β- keto esters react at lower temperatures to give the kinetic product, a β- aminoacrylate, cyclisation of which gives a 4 - quinolone. At higher temperatures, β- keto acid anilides are formed and cyclisation of these affords 2 - quinolones

The Skraup Synthesis

In this extraordinary reaction, quinoline is produced when aniline, concentrated sulfuric acid, glycerol and a mild oxidising agent are heated together. The reaction has been shown to proceed via dehydration of the glycerol to acrolein, to which aniline then adds in a conjugate fashion. Acid - catalysed cyclisation produces a 1,2 - dihydro - quinoline, finally dehydrogenated by the oxidising agent – the corresponding nitrobenzene or arsenic acid have been used classically. The Skraup synthesis is best for the ring synthesis of quinolines unsubstituted on the hetero- ring.

In principle, meta- substituted arylamines could give rise to both 5 - and 7 - substituted quinolines. In practice, electron - donating substituents direct ring closure para, thus producing 7- substituted - quinolines; meta- halo - aryl - amines produce mainly the 7 - halo - isomer. Arylamines with a strong electron – withdrawing meta- substituent give rise mainly to the 5 - substituted quinoline

N-tosyl-aniline, carrying out the conjugate addition first, the ring closure second, and the aromatisation via the elimination of toluenesulfi nate, each of the intermediates being isolated.

154

Mechanism

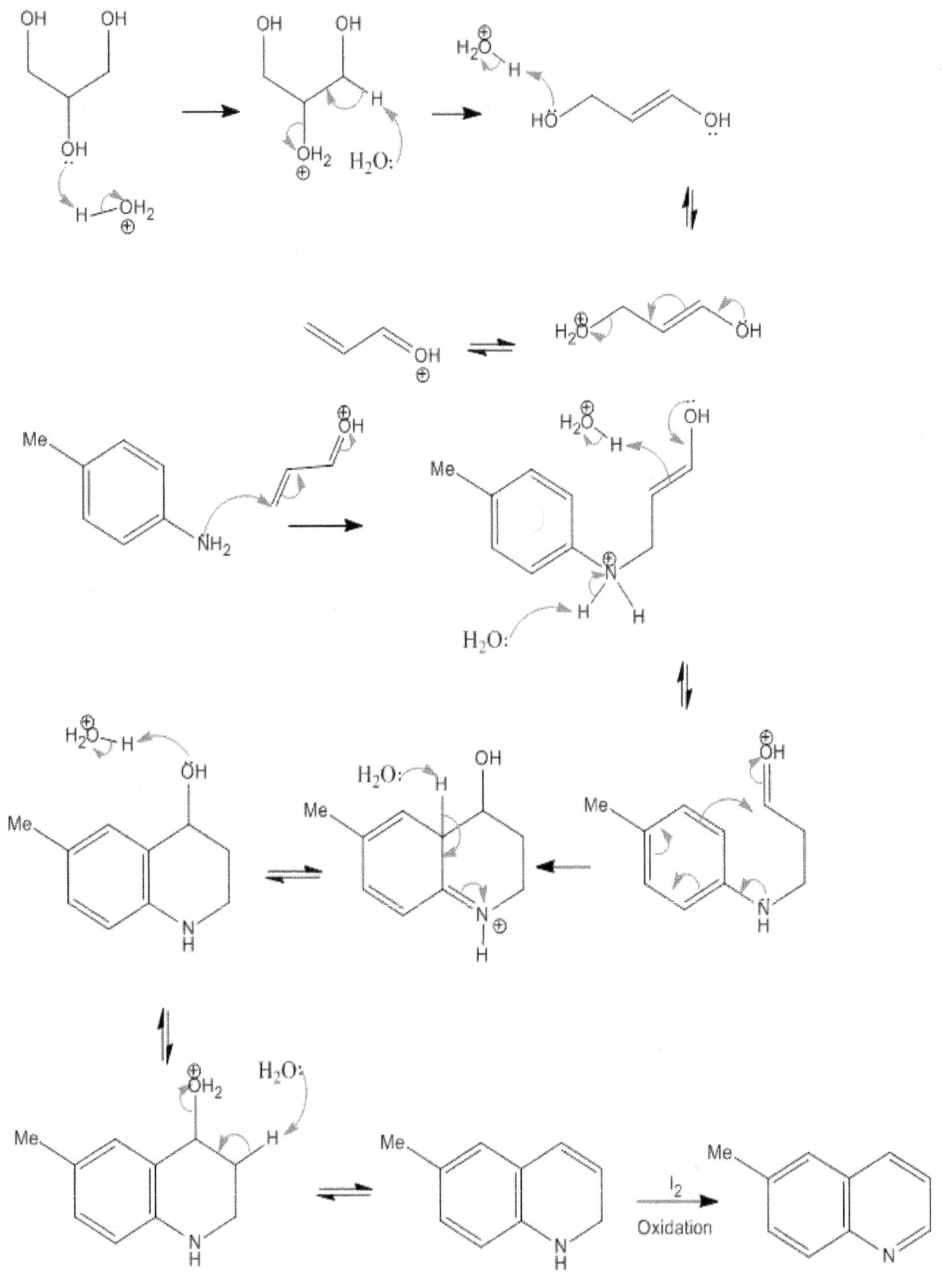
Me
I2
Oxidation

Doebner – Miller Synthesis

The use of an enone confirms the mechanism, showing that interaction of the aniline amino group with the carbonyl group is *not* the first step, and this variation is known as the Doebner – Miller synthesis.

Friedlaender Synthesis

The starting materials for this quinoline synthesis are *o*-aminoaryl aldehydes or ketones and a ketone possessing an α-methylene group. After an initial amino-ketone condensation, the intermediate undergoes base- or acid-catalyzed cyclocondensation to produce a quinoline derivative.

Mechanism

The Pfitzinger Synthesis

Hydrolysis of isatins, gives *ortho*- aminoaryl - glyoxylates, which react with ketones affording quinoline - 4 - carboxylic acids.

Mechanism

The Bischler – Napieralski Synthesis

In the classical process, a 2 - aryl - ethanamine reacts with a carboxylic acid chloride or anhydride to form an amide, which can be cyclised, with loss of water, to a 3,4 - dihydro - isoquinoline, then readily dehydrogenated to the isoquinoline using, for example, palladium, sulfur or diphenyl disulfi de.

Common cyclisation agents are phosphorus pentoxide, often with phosphoryl chloride, and phosphorus pentachloride. The electrophilic intermediate is very probably an imino chloride, or imino phosphate; the former have been isolated and treated with Lewis acids when they are converted into isonitrilium salts, which cyclise efficiently to 3,4 – dihydroisoquinolines.

In the dehydration, reagents such as PCl_5, $POCl_3$, $SOCl_2$, $ZnCl_2$ can be used to promote loss of the carbonyl oxygen. Use of $POCl_3$ leads first to formation of imidoyl phosphates in which phosphate is a good leaving group. Use of P_2O_5 or addition of P_2O_5 to a reaction with $POCl_3$ leads to pyrophosphates, which are even better leaving groups

For the cyclization, an activated arene is needed to effect ring closure at reflux temperature if the solvent is toluene. Alternatively, xylene can be used, and microwave-assisted chemistry in superheated solvents is also a viable solution.

One of the most important side reactions is the retro-Ritter reaction forming styrenes, which is also evidence for nitrilium salts as intermediates:

Ex1.

Ex2.

Ex3.